Sense Making Faith

BODY, SPIRIT, JOURNEY

Anne Richards

with the

Mission Theological Advisory Group

CHURCHES TOGETHER
IN BRITAIN AND IRELAND

Churches Together in Britain and Ireland
Bastille Court
2 Paris Garden
London SE1 8ND
www.ctbi.org.uk

ISBN 978-085169-347-7

Published 2007 by CTBI

Further copies are available from:
CTBI Publications, 4 John Wesley Road, Werrington, Peterborough PE4 6ZP
Telephone: 01733 325002
Fax: 01733 384180
sales@mph.org.uk

Enquiries regarding copyright and usage should be addressed to:
Dr Anne Richards
Mission and Public Affairs
Archbishops' Council
Church House
Great Smith Street
London
SW1P 3AZ
0207 898 1444
anne.richards@c-of-e.org.uk

Typeset in Adobe Utopia and Berthold Akzidenz Grotesque
Design and production by Makar Publishing Production, Edinburgh
Printed in Spain by Grafo Industrias Gráficas

Contents

 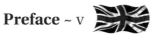

Foreword

Every so often a project comes along that does something unexpected, something that doesn't quite conform to the idea of a group getting together to do a piece of work. *Sense Making Faith* has been such a project.

It started out with a question, a question about people who construct their spiritual lives from whatever takes their fancy around them and seem perfectly happy with the results. *Why are those people happy?*

It started out with a task, the task of seeing whether the Christian faith has anything to offer today's world of spirituality shoppers and to discover what we might have forgotten about our own spiritual wisdom, richness and heritage.

It started out with a need, a need to see whether Christian mission is so bound to a particular vision of Church that it ignores the reason the words and works of Jesus are so compelling in the first place.

It started out with a decision, a decision not just to talk and write up worthy thoughts, but to work in different ways, to do things together. Early on in the project, we played a game, the game of the gift (included in the imagination chapter of this book) and found ourselves in unusual territory, laughing, miming, frowning, puzzling, wondering and dreaming. We became explorers. As time went on, we explored the Bible in new and challenging ways, met amazing people and heard their stories, discussed films, wrote poems, contemplated timeless art and wondered about the incredible creative gifts human beings bring to their investigation of the divine.

It started out.... and so did we, but it has not ended. This resource book for exploring spirituality through mind, body, spirit and journey has no conclusion, no final triumphant 'made it!' Rather, it invites us to continue exploring, making new maps of familiar places, and finding God round many unexpected corners....

We were accompanied throughout the journey by Dr Anne Richards, secretary to MTAG, who not only managed to create readable summaries of our very wide-ranging conversations but also shaped the final text. She created a space within which our meetings themselves became a spiritually enriching experience, and we give thanks to God not only for that, but for the many gifts that she brings to the wider life of the Church.

The Revd Professor John Drane
The Rt Revd Dr David Atkinson
Co-chairs of the Mission Theological Advisory Group

Preface

A Christian country?

The national census of April 2001 returned the statistic that more than seven out of ten people in the UK population said that their religion was Christian (72 per cent).[1] But other research tells us that only a very small proportion of those people actually leave their homes and go to worship regularly in a church.[2] Why do people call themselves Christian if they don't go to church? What is it about their self-understanding, their cultural understanding and their spiritual lives that makes them identify with the Christian faith?

Further, the national census also showed the presence of important other faith communities and 15.5% of the respondents claimed to have no religious allegiance. But studies[3] also tell us that even those people who do not identify with any particular faith have spiritual lives, which develop in particular ways, but which often they do not share in any systematic way.

Apologetics and mission

This book is first of all for Christians who are genuinely interested in the spirituality of other people, many of whom have no connection with Church, and it is also for all those who are interested in what God is doing in their lives and in the lives of others. In what follows, 'we' refers to Christians who are still within the tradition of churchgoing. This book will seek to engage 'us' and the traditions we share within the activity of worship, prayer and fellowship together with those others who are exploring faith beyond our traditions because we are exploring faith too. Christians are called upon to proclaim the good news of the gospel and to share our faith with others and witness to its importance and centrality in our own lives. The time-honoured term for presenting and explaining the Christian faith is 'apologetics', but this book asks if we need to find other means of reaching out to people, being alongside them and finding common threads and bridges between their lives and ours. We will look at some of the implications of those bridges and what they do to affect our faith and our spiritual journey. In this book we will investigate the language of the senses, body languages, in order to seek shared understanding between our own faith and those of other faiths and none. We will try to see what implications those bridges have for the mission of the whole Church.

We can say at once that it is an important part of the mission task because those people beyond the Church are, like us, wayfarers on spiritual paths. But there are many things we may not know or understand about these fellow travellers. What language of God do they speak? What stories do they have to tell? Does our traditional way of sharing the gospel of Jesus Christ and teaching people the faith have any relevance for people who are busy defining their spiritual lives for themselves?

God of surprises

To do this, we have looked at the spiritual journey that we as Christians are engaged upon, as a spiral path of discovery broadening out from scripture, reason, tradition and experience and moving into new and unknown places where Christ is always ready to surprise us. The Archbishop of Canterbury has said, in commissioning evangelists: 'the kind of discovery that you'll make again and again in your ministry (is) of the surprising presence of Christ in places where you thought he hadn't gone before you'.[4] At the same time, we become aware of others moving in another spiral, close to ours, moving from different, perhaps more vague, spiritual centres and closing in to where God leads them, and perhaps elsewhere. What bridges connect our path with theirs? What do we have to say to, and learn from, each other? One of the things we have found in doing this work is that the journey takes us into places of spiritual discovery, but often what we discover is not completely new, but a rediscovery of the riches of the Christian tradition. One of God's surprises for us has been the words and works of the mystics, of Christian saints, of the mothers and fathers of the early Church – all of which often already describe what we find if we only pay a little more attention to the world we live in.

The double spiral

This image of the spiral is found all over the creation, whether within the cosmos or our extraordinary world. Telescopes show us the breathtaking beauty of spiral galaxies, but we also find spirals in flowers, shells, animal horns. The spiral was for ancient people the most basic form of the labyrinth. So we can imagine our spiritual journeys as a spiral pathway like that of a leaf stem or a shell, with all of us passing up and down the spirals. At another level, the double spiral becomes the double helix, the mysterious pattern at the heart of our genetic being.

Choosing an image of a pattern which is deeply inscribed into the 'genesis' of nature, we have also chosen an organic focus and process for our book. We have gone back to basics and asked: what does it mean to be a human being, now, today, in a society like ours? We are embodied people. Inextricably bound up with sophisticated reason and intellectual arguments, and inseparable from the constructions of faith, we receive experience, information and sensation through every part of our bodies. We are embodied minds and interpreted bodies. What is it our bodies tell us and how does this experience of the daily life of being human actually inform our spiritual lives in the deepest part of our sense of being alive? How do the senses help us find our way down the path of spiritual discovery?

Sensing the world

To answer these questions this book conducts an investigation into the world of the senses. Each chapter looks at what the Church has in its own tradition about the senses and then look at how the senses are engaged in the society in which we live. Where are the gaps and where are the important connections and contradictions? Often people are rediscovering things we have known and treasured as part of our faith all

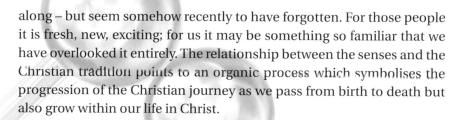

along – but seem somehow recently to have forgotten. For those people it is fresh, new, exciting; for us it may be something so familiar that we have overlooked it entirely. The relationship between the senses and the Christian tradition points to an organic process which symbolises the progression of the Christian journey as we pass from birth to death but also grow within our life in Christ.

Spiral journeys

Each chapter of this book is a separate spiral journey, focusing on one of the body's senses. To guide our thoughts and ideas we asked the Archbishop of Canterbury, Dr Rowan Williams, if he would offer us a creative meditation for each of the chapters on the senses. He has responded by sending us six haiku. A haiku is a poem, based on an ancient Japanese tradition of poetry, which is set out in 17 syllables in the space of three lines. The economy of each poem means that every word has layers of meaning and asks the reader to engage deeply and imaginatively with the world it invokes.

The Archbishop's haiku, then, sets the scene for the first part of an ongoing conversation we want to have with the churchgoing Christian reader. Each chapter also then contains suggestions about how the tradition of the Church has engaged that particular sense and we invite our readers to see how it is relevant for them today as part of Christian witness. We then go on to look at people on different, but intertwined, spiritual journeys – how the same senses are stimulated and excited through contemporary culture and we then look for relevant connections. Most of all we want people to *have* experiences without the expectation of a particular outcome or end point and to share these with others as a beginning of mutual exchange, wonder and delight. *How* we have these experiences matters, because all too often people can, in T. S. Eliot's words, 'have the experience but miss the meaning'.

It is important to remember that we never have uninterpreted experiences: even toothache has to be understood *as* toothache (rather than, say, as a pain somewhere in the head). We often say that we 'attach' significance to events or experiences, but this is not really right. As soon as we notice that we experience something, it is already significant to us. The significance does not come later, as a result of a separate process of 'attaching'. To have an experience is to find it significant in some way. The crucial point is that *how* we have experiences can change. Our experiences can be transformed, deepened, filled with new surprise and delight, by learning new languages, or by engaging with contexts and histories more fully. Christian life is about transformation and healing. We might expect, then, that living a Christian life may mean the discovery of transformation and healing in how we engage and are engaged by our sense experiences. One of the exciting things about the spiral journey and paying attention to our world through our senses, is finding that we experience the familiar differently. This makes us wonder and dream and stirs a desire to find out what God is doing. In this process begins the seeds of an evangelism which takes the spirituality of people outside the Church seriously and seeks to learn from them.

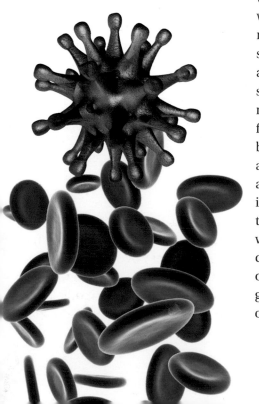

At the same time, each journey explores what we learn from those who lack the different physical senses, what happens when such senses are abused and how the senses can be used in the healing process.

Each chapter's journey also contains questions, activities, scripture passages, prayers, pictures and poetry and ways of providing a range of engagement. However, this book is only one way in, a starting point for the task of sharing faith with others who would walk with us, if only for a little way. Our accompanying website contains more suggestions, resources and opportunity for feedback (www.spiritualjourneys.org. uk).

More about us

The Mission Theological Advisory Group was created as a partnership between the Churches' Commission on Mission (now Global Mission Network) of Churches Together in Britain and Ireland and the General Synod's Board of Mission (now the Mission and Public Affairs Division of the Archbishops' Council of the Church of England) in 1992. Its purpose is to advise the Christian churches on matters affecting the mission of the whole Church. In particular, MTAG has become known for its work on Christian mission in relation to our contemporary culture. MTAG has published *The Search for Faith and the Witness of the Church* in 1996, and *Presence and Prophecy*, together with a study guide, *Transparencies, pictures of mission through prayer and reflection* in 2002.

Since 2002, the membership of the group for this project has been as follows:

The Rt Revd Dr David Atkinson, (co-chair);
The Revd Professor John Drane (co-chair);
Dr Nicholas Adams;
Mr Simon Barrow (to 2005);
Mr Andrew Brookes;
The Rt Revd Dr Brian Castle;
The Revd Canon Dr Graham Kings;
The Revd Joanna Penberthy;
Canon Janice Price (from 2005);
Dr Anne Richards (secretary);
The Revd Dr Israel Selvanayagam;
The Revd Dr David Spriggs (consultant);
The Revd Dr Andrew Wood.

More information about the individual members of the group is found at the end of this book and on the website www.spiritualjourneys.org

How to use this book

Each chapter in this book is set out in the form of a journey. The journey spirals out from its Christian centre, concentrating on one of the physical senses. It encounters both the loss of that sense and the abuse of that sense, before journeying back again through the activities and insights of people outside the Church. Each chapter progresses through its double-spiral seeking to make connections in which we understand other people better and find new and appropriate ways of sharing the gospel.

The journeys are there for you to take at your own pace. There is no 'right' place to end up, no set of recommendations or requirements involved in the process. The purpose of each journey is to focus on what it means to be a human being under God, and to begin to see bridges to, and connections with, the spirituality of those who do not locate themselves within the Christian faith, or who perhaps are drifting on the edges of it. In those connections are the seeds of a form of mission which helps make sense of where people already are. What you do with those seeds depends on what is appropriate in your own situation; where and whether you sow them and nurture them is up to you.

It is difficult to represent such a journey of exploration in the typical format of a book. For this reason, each chapter will have text to read and illustrations to look at and these combine to describe the journey. However, throughout the text there will be points where you are invited to pause reading the text and concentrate on an activity. These different activities are like waystations on the journey, where you can, if you wish, change the pace of the journey and stop and engage more deeply in what the text has been discussing. These waystations on the journey include pauses for prayer, pauses for reflection, pauses for meditation, and pauses which invite you to put the book down altogether and go off and do something.

Each waystation on the journey is marked by an icon, which tells you that a pause has been reached. The various things to do are then shown by text in red.

A waystation for prayer is shown like this: **Prayer Point**

A waystation for reflection is shown like this: **Reflection Point**

A waystation for meditation is shown like this **Meditation Point**

A waystation which involves doing something looks like this: **Activity Point**

While the waystations help you to draw breath and go deeper into the journey, you can move on if you want to and come back to them at a later time.

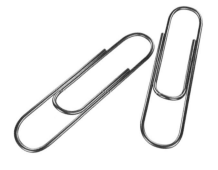

In addition, there are questions embedded in the text at various points to give you more things to think about. Each journey is followed by a summary of the chapter's themes and ideas, enabling you to look back at the whole journey and to help you decide if you want to revisit any of the material.

In various places you will also see this icon . This means that there is additional material about the topics under discussion on our website, www.spiritualjourneys.org.uk, where you will find even more material to pursue further journeys, with links to more pictures, information and ideas.

Using this book as part of a group: note to group leaders

Each chapter in this book is set out for a reader to use as a personal journey, but we have also included further material at the end of the book (Exploring the Journey Points Together, p. 125) which allows it to be studied and enjoyed by groups of people together. This extra material is designed to help a group leader, or leaders, plan and lead a session on each chapter's material. By using the extra material for group work, *Sense Making Faith* could be used as a Lent or Advent course, or by house groups, church groups, fellowship groups, ecumenical groups and school groups. The emphasis in the group work is on play and exploration, and the group session based on the introductory material is set out as a mini-journey in itself. There is plenty of stuff for all ages and if you wish you can select what kinds of activities are best for your group from each section. There are even more ideas about group work and more downloadable resources on the website.

The Garden of Earthly Delights.
Outer panel of an interactive triptych
by Hieronymous Bosch, *c.*1500.

Sense Making Faith
BODY, SPIRIT, JOURNEY

Introduction to the Journey

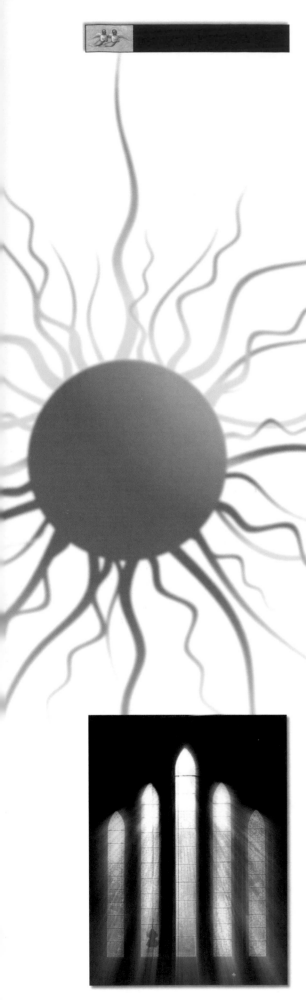

Themes and engagement

This is an introduction not only to the themes of this book, but also to the way we want to engage with the subject matter. So first of all, have a look at this image of a statue built long ago to impress on people the power and might of an ancient god.

What's out there: the wonders of the world

This represents one of the seven ancient wonders of the world, the Colossus of Rhodes, a giant statue of the sun god Helios that stood at the entrance to the harbour. The others were: the great pyramid of Giza, the hanging gardens of Babylon, the statue of Zeus at Olympia, the Temple of Artemis at Ephesus, the Mausoleum at Halicarnassus, and the Lighthouse of Alexandria. From ancient times, people have laboured (often across generations) to produce great monuments to honour, celebrate and witness to their faith in something divine, beyond and behind everyday life. Yet both gods and monuments disappear, so what is it that truly endures? Christians would say that the incarnate God cannot be lost because in Christ he has become as we are and we ourselves have become living stones. Others outside the Church will often point to the enduring and renewing cycles and seasons of nature as something on which to depend.

We can also think of monuments today which evoke a numinous sense of something Other, not quite realising how the understanding of both creation and incarnation come together. For many, the great cathedrals may come to mind, for others, the ancient sacred stones of Stonehenge may provoke awe and wonder. Stonehenge is famous for being carefully constructed and oriented in line with the sun, but many churches and cathedrals also have this quality. Churches were typically built in the east-west axis, so that the rising sun (and Risen Son) would shine in upon the altar through the great East Window. People have always been buried with their faces towards the returning sun. In Vézelay, in France, for example, the cathedral is designed so the sun shines upon different saints on their actual feast days. One of the things we may have forgotten is that churches were always designed to fit within and harmonise with God's creation, using sunlight and the rhythms of nature to remind us of Christ as light of the world who has come to banish the darkness and illuminate human life forever. 🌐

Many ancient wonders of the world are gone now, but, through human technology and imaginative ability there are surely many more to come just around the corner. What will they look like, and will they teach us about spiritual matters?

Go For A Walk

Go out and look at any local buildings or monuments that especially interest you. If you have a camera, you could take some photos. Some questions to think about are:

❖ **Are there any amazing places, buildings, monuments, things you've seen or experienced? What's wonderful about them?**

❖ **What could you find in or around your church to catch people's attention? Why would they stop and stare? Why would they take a photo?**

❖ **How does *your* church relate to the natural world outside its walls? Could such links be strengthened or enhanced?**

The works of human hands can be truly amazing and can fill us with awe,[1] but what about the even more amazing works of God's hands? How often do we stop to wonder at the beauty and diversity of creation and about the extraordinary nature of any human being? The former bishop of Oxford, the Rt Revd Richard Harries, has suggested that we should read the phrase in Ephesians 2:10 as 'we are his works of art'. Many TV programmes involve medical and crime dramas about the vulnerability and fragility of the human body, but where do we remember to celebrate the amazing construction, workings and capabilities of the human body as a spiritual experience rather than a biology lesson? Professor Robert Winston made a series of creative and instructive programmes called *The Human Body*, but we may also begin to think about how we are 'fearfully and wonderfully made' (Psalm 139:14) if we only watch sport. Ice skaters and dancers, athletes (from tiny gymnasts to huge weight-lifters), footballers, swimmers or skiers can all remind us of the precision and skill our bodies are capable of.

A point of reflection from Thomas Traherne

You never enjoy the world aright, till the Sea itself floweth in your veins, till you are clothed with the heavens and crowned with the stars: and perceive yourself to be the sole heir of the whole world, and more than so, because men are in it who are every one sole heirs as well as you. Till you can sing and rejoice and delight in God, as misers do in gold, and Kings in sceptres, you never enjoy the world.

Centuries I–29

Being human

Like the seven ancient wonders of the world, all the things we construct wear out, crumble away and pass into memory, but human beings are also wonders of the world. Through our embodiment as creatures of flesh, blood and bone we too stand as monuments to the Divine. But as creatures we are not 'designed' or 'made' as statues for contemplation,

for what is truly wonderful about ourselves as embodied creatures is that through our bodies we can engage with God's world and interact with it and with each other.[2] So if we are going to think of ourselves as wonders of God's world, we must think about the extraordinary gift of our senses.

Through our physical senses we access the world and make sense of it, and large parts of our brain are given over to this sensing and sense-making process. This is no less true for people with disability – the loss of one or more senses can mean the brain compensates in other areas, giving people a more rich and refined experience in other ways. Even people with (to us) very severe impairment can sometimes show they have treasures of experience inaccessible to the rest of us, finding mystery and wonder in numbers, music, colour, and the worlds of the imagination. The experience of each of us is constructed out of our different ways of accessing the world and our deep spiritual core develops according to what we do with that experience. For example, even a relatively small loss, such as colour-blindness, can open up new worlds and ways of seeing and understanding. The neurologist Oliver Sacks talks about an artist, who having lost his ability to see, recognise or even remember colour, learned to realise that his different sight now allowed him to 'see' things, like sunsets, in ways not experienced by other people and to share his new vision by painting them.[3]

Meanwhile, we can be so used to the luxury of our senses that we take them for granted. Brian Keenan, deprived of stimulation in his Lebanese prison cell reminds us of the joy and wonder our physical senses should bring us if we weren't so complacent about having them:

The fruits, the colours mesmerize me in a quiet rapture that spins through my head. I am entranced by colour. I lift an orange into the flat filthy palm of my hand and feel and smell and lick it. The colour orange, the colour, My God the colour orange. Before me is a feast of colour. I feel myself begin to dance, slowly. …

…I sit in quiet joy, so complete, beyond the meaning of joy. My soul finds its own completeness in that bowl of colour.[4]

This experience may remind us of Mother Julian of Norwich when she contemplated a hazelnut:

In this vision he showed me a little thing, the size of a hazelnut, and it was round as a ball. I looked at it with the eye of my understanding and thought 'What may this be?' And it was generally answered thus: 'It is all that is made.' I marvelled how it might last, for it seemed it might suddenly have sunk into nothing because of its littleness. And I was answered in my understanding: 'It lasts and ever shall, because God loves it.'[5] 🌐

Perhaps it is time to recover the wonder of inhabiting our physical bodies and the life of the senses in order to see, as Brian Keenan and Mother Julian saw, the extraordinary nature of God's world around us.

He gave us eyes to see them and lips that we might tell
How great is God almighty that has made all things well.

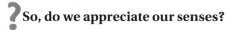 **So, do we appreciate our senses?**

Have a look at *Equilibrium*

If you can't find a copy of this film, here is a brief description:

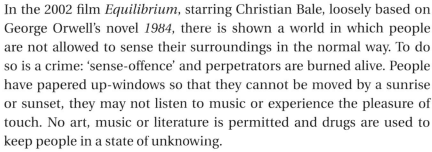

In the 2002 film *Equilibrium*, starring Christian Bale, loosely based on George Orwell's novel *1984*, there is shown a world in which people are not allowed to sense their surroundings in the normal way. To do so is a crime: 'sense-offence' and perpetrators are burned alive. People have papered up-windows so that they cannot be moved by a sunrise or sunset, they may not listen to music or experience the pleasure of touch. No art, music or literature is permitted and drugs are used to keep people in a state of unknowing.

Interestingly, this state of affairs is perpetrated by a 'Father' who represents the Grammaton (the Tetragrammaton is the sacred name of God in the Hebrew Scriptures: YHWH, or Yahweh) and whose enforcers are called 'clerics'. The story is about one of the highest clerics who smashes his vial of suppressor drug by accident and so rediscovers the world of the senses as if for the first time. What is interesting in this film, is the way attention is drawn to things we take for granted: the touch of a cold metal railing occasions wonder; the cleric weeps when he hears a piece of music by Beethoven. He tears down his window-paper and gazes hungrily at the sky. He experiences love and anguish as a woman he loves is taken away to be burned alive. In the end he becomes the one who must depose the 'Father' and liberate people into again becoming fully alive.

The film asks us an important question about our ability to share our faith and about our mission. Have we, like the 'Father' and the clerics in the film, failed to encourage people to appreciate the gift of being alive? Do people see the Church as a place where the joy of feeling is suppressed? Are clerics the suppressors of people's happiness? People outside the Church do in fact quite often make this claim.

 But is this what God wants or intends?

They want you to come and do their sessions ...they are saying, 'Do you have any questions about God?' 'No, I've just come here to play with my child.'[6]

Reflection on being fully alive

St Irenaeus tells us: 'the glory of God is a living man; and the life of man consists in beholding God' which is usually expressed today as: 'The joy of God is a human being fully alive and the life of a human being consists in beholding God.'[7]

❖ **Do people see Christians as human beings who are 'fully alive'?**

The senses in scripture

Seeing

The physical senses are all important in the formation of the relationships between Jesus and those who came to believe in him. People flocked to see Jesus – it was important to have actual sight of his physical person. In the story of Zacchaeus (Luke 19:1–10), we hear how Zacchaeus climbed the tree in order to have sight of Jesus himself and how his efforts were rewarded by Jesus' seeing him and through that seeing and recognition, making it possible for them to meet and eat together, leading to conversion and change of life. Seeing and recognising Jesus is therefore a fundamental of Christian life. Jesus is not only a physical human presence, but also the fundamental sacred sign of God with us. Christians continue to carry with them through history visual images of Jesus' physical person.

? What visual signs of Jesus do you have in your home and at church? Who sees them? How could you get more people to see them?

Hearing

We also know that people came from miles around to hear Jesus and to respond to his words. Listening to Jesus' voice is therefore significant in the Gospels. People listened to Jesus' words, took them into their hearts and allowed that listening to become the foundation for the way to live life and search for God. So today, hearing and responding to the words of Jesus remains significant for the missionary enterprise. So too the words of Jesus become the sacred message of God to the created order. Christians cherish their scripture with the words of Jesus retained in them. For many people watching the film *The Passion of the Christ*, the dialogue in Aramaic brought home the sense of Jesus as a person with his own language, dialect and manner of speech.

? How do you hear the words of Jesus? How can others hear them for themselves?

Touching

Touch is also profoundly important. Touching Jesus is seen as access to his healing power and also to the physical reality of the resurrection, as Thomas is invited to touch the wounds. Thus the real interaction of Jesus with things that have gone terribly wrong in people's lives, such as sickness, disadvantage and death, shows us that we too have access to transformation and healing in our lives. Christians have at different times invested importance in touchable things such as relics and in things supposed to be touched by Jesus such as holy shrouds and napkins. This has also given rise to the power of the grail legend and its association with holiness and healing.

? In what ways do people experience Jesus' touch today? What things happen in your church to make it possible for them to do so?

Moreover, it is important to recognise that this access to Jesus via the human senses is continuous both through his life and after his resurrection. The resurrection appearances stress that the same contact is possible: the resurrection event is real. Jesus can be seen and recognised as a human person after his death. He speaks and can be heard; he can be touched and encountered.

Tasting and Smelling

Taste and smell also come together in the presence of Jesus. Encounter with Jesus as sign, message and transformation come often in the context of shared eating and drinking. Zacchaeus changes his life around, for example, at a meal with Jesus. Jesus also reminds us to think of heaven in terms of being called to a feast. So eating and drinking, with its attendant smelling and tasting, is identified with Jesus' actual physical body by his command. At the Last Supper, the disciples are told to eat and drink bread and wine and to know it as Jesus' own Body and Blood. In the Eucharist all the senses are therefore to be employed in meeting and knowing Jesus.

? **When we celebrate the Eucharist what do the elements taste and smell like? Can we get across to others the rich sensory experience of the Last Supper?**

Loss of the senses

Along with this, Jesus' ministry is characterised by healing people whose senses had been lost. In part this is a prophetic and messianic statement of who Jesus is (eg the message to John the Baptist in Luke 7:22) and it is used by the Gospel writers as such, but this is not to suggest that those who are or who become sense impaired are designated less than fully human by Jesus' actions. Rather such people become illustrators of the *importance* of seeing, hearing and touching Jesus. If you can see, you become complacent about being able to see. If you lose your sight and have it restored, you are in the best position to appreciate its miraculous potential and quality. So those who are healed by Jesus are significant for the new born-again experience of encountering Jesus through the senses and calling people's attention to the importance of using our senses to experience the wonder and power of God's greatness and glory as we see in the paralysed man who takes up his bed in Luke 5:25.

It is true for us too. As Christians we can become all too complacent about the way we encounter Jesus. So we need to learn from those who are blind, deaf, or otherwise sense impaired to remind us that we must use our physical abilities with humility and awareness. The following chapters will contain illustrations which help us to reflect on this.

To begin to get ready for the journeys into the world of the senses, let us focus on a passage of scripture that is probably familiar and see how all the senses have a role to play in telling us something about Jesus in fellowship with those he loves.

Reflection: John 12:1–8

Six days before the Passover Jesus came to Bethany, the home of Lazarus, whom he had raised from the dead. There they gave a dinner for him. Martha served, and Lazarus was one of those at the table with him. Mary took a pound of costly perfume made of pure nard, anointed Jesus' feet, and wiped them with her hair. The house was filled with the fragrance of the perfume. But Judas Iscariot, one of his disciples (the one who was about to betray him), said 'why was this perfume not sold for three hundred denarii and the money given to the poor?' (He said this not because he cared about the poor, but because he was a thief; he kept the common purse and used to steal what was put into it.) Jesus said, 'Leave her alone. She bought it so that she might keep it for the day of my burial. You always have the poor with you, but you do not always have me.'

In this passage of John we are given an extraordinarily rich and detailed picture of intimacy. It is the more extraordinary for its context in the gospel. The bigger picture is the plot against Jesus' life and this story is followed by his entry into Jerusalem, with the crowds shouting 'Hosanna'. Complex politics and great events lie all around, preparing for the scenes with which we are all familiar from Holy Week and Easter. But into the middle of this is slotted another preparation scene, which apart from its function as a sign of Jesus' preparation for his death, carries a great deal more.

This little scene tells us much about the physical life of Jesus and requires us to look at what it means to be human and to be alive and in relationship with others. This scene also carries great stress on the participation of the human senses. The passage draws our eyes in, from the landscape of the town, to the house, to the room with the dinner table, to the people around it and in the room and then focuses down to specific parts of the persons involved in an act of service and love: Jesus' feet and Mary's hair. We are asked to see all this in greater and greater detail. There is a conversation we are expected to hear: Judas' protest and Jesus' rebuke to him. There is a dinner, the participants are eating and drinking, tasting and enjoying food. This is not given to us as an abstract fact, rather we have to imagine Martha in the act of serving the food and Lazarus, whose senses were once lost forever, is there participating fully in human life. He, too, is eating and drinking with the Son of God.

Even so, the senses of smell and touch are paramount. The 'house is filled with the fragrance of the perfume', an extravagance of scent bringing with it its memory of death and burial, extraordinarily evocative in a family where death had been turned to life by Jesus' presence and Jesus' word, and within this cloud of fragrance is the intimate act of the anointing. Mary has direct contact with Jesus' body. It is a contact which may not be broken, an intimacy which binds the fellowship of love together.

? What other passages of scripture can you think of, in which sense experiences are important?

Prayer from St Teresa of Avila

Lord Christ,
You have no body on earth but ours,
No hands but ours,
No feet but ours.
Ours are the eyes through which your compassion must look out on
    the world.
Ours are the feet by which you may still
go about doing good.
Ours are the hands with which
you bless people now.
Bless our minds and bodies, that we may be a blessing to others.
Amen

John 12:1–8 also points to an important aspect of our journeys into the world of the senses. In meeting Jesus through the senses we will find that we are drawn to the feast with him, that we are drawn to respond to him, to become involved in acts of love, to *worship*.

Where have we been?

This introductory chapter has asked us to think about what it means to be a human being equipped with physical senses, and how being human and sensing the world is also important in scripture.

❖ The wonders of the world, old and new, can fill us with amazement. Great buildings and natural wonders can also point us towards something more than the here and now, a sense of God, or of the transcendent.

❖ Human beings are also amazing. The way human biology works is astonishing and should similarly fill us with wonder. Our physical senses are extraordinary and give us access to a rich and varied experience of the world.

❖ People who lose one or more of their senses sometimes find that their other physical senses become more acute and can tell us more about the depth and richness of a sense-environment.

❖ Being deprived of our senses can reduce our humanity and make us lose touch with reality, as in the experiences of hostages and prisoners.

❖ Scripture also tells us about the importance of the physical senses. Many scriptural passages invite us to think about the gift of sight, hearing, smell, touch and taste, and by these means enhance our appreciation and immersion in bible stories.

❖ In the story of the anointing of Jesus' feet, sense descriptions and impressions are particularly important, reminding us of the physical incarnate presence of Jesus.

Psalm 139:13–14

For it was you who formed my inward parts;
You knit me together in my mother's womb.
I praise you, for I am fearfully and wonderfully made.
Wonderful are your works;
That I know very well.

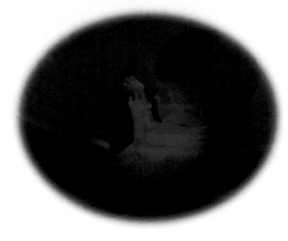

A million arrows, I
the target, where the lines meet
and are knotted

Archbishop Rowan Williams

Journey into Seeing

> **Of all the senses, sight must be the most delightful.**
> Helen Keller

Starting the journey: what is seeing?

The first step in this journey requires us to think about our eyes and the miracle of seeing. How much of the world is really accessible to us through sight?

In the classic science fiction novel by Frank Herbert, *Dune*, the Bible of the distant future carries a text which becomes important to Paul Atreides, the novel's prophet/messiah/martyr: *What senses do we lack that we cannot see another world all around us?*

When we think about the physical sense of sight, we often assume that the whole of the created order is accessible to us, but it is not. In fact only a small part of it is accessible to human beings without other aids. We need telescopes to see the breathtaking loveliness of God's cosmos beyond the pinpricks of stars visible to the naked eye. We need microscopes to penetrate down to the worlds of the very small, uncovering life and activity we could never know had existed.

Our eyes are sensitive to the range of visible light, the colours of the rainbow which form the covenant promise to Noah. So everything we can see and embrace with our eyes is included in God's promise to us. But other sighted animals can see aspects of the creation that we cannot. Many have eyes that are not only better constructed than ours, but provide better vision. For example, Richard Dawkins points out that 'tetrachromatic turtles, for example, might be most disappointed by the unrealistic (to them) pictures on our television and cinema screens'.[1] Predators often have acute vision to see small moving creatures: 'the eyes of a hawk'. Some insects are sensitive to ultraviolet light and see flowers brilliantly illuminated, glowing against a dark background. Some nocturnal animals have acute night vision, so that what to us is a pitch black forest is for them a living landscape. Other animals appear to construct pictures out of other radiation. Bats 'see' by sonar, some fish use electric fields, others magnetic fields. In the dark places of the world where light does not penetrate, such as the depths of the ocean, animals still 'see'. The created order is full of eyes and ways of seeing, so that we need to start by realising that what we can see is a very small part of all there is to see and know. Quantum physics tells us there are some things we can never 'see', because the act of seeing, using light, alters the reality of the quantum world. In terms of the world as God sees and knows it, we are very blind indeed.

Think about these lines from a hymn

Immortal, invisible, God only wise
In light inaccessible hid from our eyes

Light a candle.

Look hard at the flame. What colour is it? What shape does the flame take? How does it change? What does the flame remind you of? What is hidden by the brightness of the flame?

Moving out: glimpsing God in our time

Look around!

In a famous phrase St Paul reminds us that 'now we see through a glass darkly', but in heaven we shall see God face to face, as he really is. The suggestion is very much that what we see and experience now is only a part of the true reality. Similarly, if we pay attention to the idea that there is more to see, we can become aware of the numinous in nature and in people and things around us. We become aware of the work of the Spirit and glimpses of the *doxa*, the glory of God.

In scripture, we learn more of how the glory of God bursts into the world. And we notice that the great teachers, prophets and messengers of God's people are those whose eyes are open and whose attention is caught by the revelation of God's glory in unlikely places. Moreover, God's glory appears not to the great kings and wealthy leaders, but often to the humble and obedient people who, not distracted by finery or luxury, remember to keep their eyes open and their awareness sharp. The story of Balaam's ass (Numbers 22) is a reminder to us of what we can miss if we don't pay attention to the signs God is putting before us. Moses' attention is caught by the burning bush, flaming, but not burning up (Exodus 3:2). Ezekiel is overwhelmed by his extraordinary vision of wheels and eyes (Ezekiel 1:4ff). In the birth narratives, the shepherds are amazed by the angelic vision (Luke 2:9), the wise men by a star in the sky (Matthew 2:2). The revelation of St John the Divine (the Apocalypse), is characterised by acts of visionary seeing. The word 'behold!' is more than an invitation to have a look; it is an invitation to pay close attention to what we can see of God's work.

The spiritual journey can be characterised by moments of vision and seeing God in places where we would not expect to see or find him. We can become aware of the numinous nature of particular places, when the world seems to be visually transformed. We can see Christ in others, recognise him and greet him. We may discern the work of the Spirit flaming out from things we encounter around us. But there is another side to this: failing to see God.

King of Kings Statue, Solid Rock Church, Ohio, USA.

Reflect on David Jones' *A, a, a, Domine Deus*[2]

I have tired the eyes of the mind
    regarding the colours and lights.
I have felt for His Wounds
    in nozzles and containers.
I have wondered for the automatic devices.
I have tested the inane patterns
    without prejudice.
I have been on my guard
    not to condemn the unfamiliar.
For it is easy to miss Him
    at the turn of a civilisation.

? **Do you agree with David Jones about how it can be hard to see God in our time? Are there times in your life as a Christian when you have missed God?**

? Clearly, we must pay more attention in order to see God at work in the world. But who else is seeing that work and what do they make of it? And can our own eyes deceive us?

Reflect on a Fraser Spiral

Start at the red dot and try to follow the path round to the centre. Don't read on until you've tried it.

This is an optical illusion called the Fraser Spiral.[3] When you look at this image you see a spiral. But it is not, it is actually a series of circles. Your brain can't make sense of the shapes in the interrupted sections of the circle and rearranges things to make a 'best fit' spiral pathway. Optical illusions help us to realise that seeing and making sense can be two different things. What does it take to 'make sense' of God?

? At what times does our spiral spiritual journey towards a deeper relationship with God and witness to others end up as going round in a closed circle?

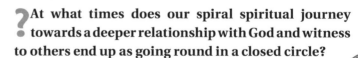

Being in God's sight

As Christians, one of the things we have to think about in relationship to seeing, perception and discernment, is to think about how people outside our faith see us, and how indeed God sees us. If we are to reach out in our spiritual journey and encounter those others who are seeking and searching, what will they see in us and what will God see of our work to share his news?

Prayer: Hebrews 13:20–1

Now may the God of peace,
who brought back from the dead our Lord Jesus,
the great shepherd of the sheep,
by the blood of the eternal covenant,
make you complete in everything good
so that you may do his will,
working among us that which is pleasing in his sight,
through Jesus Christ to whom be the glory for ever and ever.
Amen

Journey beyond seeing: being blind

It is a terrible thing to see and have no vision.

Helen Keller

In continuing on our journey in what it means to have eyes and have sight, we must reach a point where we consider what it is for eyes to fail and to have no vision. When we can see, we are always in danger of over-looking things that are important: there's none so blind as those that will not see. Very few of us will enjoy perfect eyesight throughout our lives and some of us will fall victim to diseases which cause us to go blind. Moreover, we can learn much from the experiences of people born blind whose experience of the world is so different from ours and yet not filled with the kind of complacency we can fall into about the way we see our world. For example:

When a blind church organist in Norfolk was reading the lesson at the Christmas carol service from Braille, he stopped and apologised that he was reading slowly because 'his hands were too cold'.

As Christians, it is easy to use 'sighted' language to talk about God. The Bible is full of 'light' and 'seeing' language. Israel is to be a light to the nations; Jesus is the 'light of the world'; we are supposed to light our lamps and shine as a witness to others. Many of our hymns use such 'seeing' language – 'walk, walk, in the light'. Yet the blind theologian John Hull reminds us that for him, as in the title of one of his books: *In the Beginning There Was Darkness*.[4] The neurologist Oliver Sacks writes of reading Hull's book *Touching the Rock*: 'Two years after becoming completely blind, Hull had apparently become so non-visual as to resemble someone who had been blind from birth. In a profoundly religious way, and in language sometimes reminiscent of that of St John of the Cross, Hull has entered into this state, surrendered himself with a sort of acquiescence and joy. And such "deep" blindness he conceives as "an authentic and autonomous world, a place of its own... Being a whole-body seer is to be in one of the concentrated human conditions."'[5] John Hull also reminds us that images of blindness often become attached to ideas of sin or being lost. Redemption and restoration are concepts linked to the restoration of sight:

**There is in God (some say)
A deep and dazzling darkness**

Henry Vaughan

Amazing Grace!
How sweet the sound
That saved a wretch like me.
I once was lost, but now am found,
Was blind, but now I see.

'the blind receive their sight'
Matthew 11:5

'let me see again'
Mark 10:51

Yet scripture also couples blindness and the discovery of God in an interesting way. In order to find and encounter God, people often have to learn *not* to see. Away from visual distraction, spiritual wayfarers can find themselves in the presence of the living God.

Moses for example, encounters God in the darkness of storms (eg Exodus 19:16) and in the pillar of cloud (eg Exodus 33:9). Within such darkness, Moses is able to enter into a deeper covenant relationship with God and convey God's will to the people. Saul's conversion on the road to Damascus takes place in what is probably another storm and leaves him blind until Ananias lays hands on him and calls him into his new life: '"Brother Saul, the Lord Jesus, who appeared to you on your way here, has sent me so that you may regain your sight and be filled with the Holy Spirit." And immediately something like scales fell from his eyes, and his sight was restored.' (Acts 9:17–18). A profound darkness and storm falls over the land when Jesus dies.

The restoration of sight is therefore something much more than just the capacity to see again. Within blindness and darkness there can be a profound encounter with divine power, one which is translated into witness and worship. The blind people who are healed by Jesus first encounter him within their blindness. It is here that the journey of faith is completed – and affirmed by their new sight. That sight is the sight of faith, the other side of their spiritual journey. So we may miss the significance and power of the word 'see' when Fanny Crosby, the blind hymn-writer, writes in her famous hymn 'To God be the glory' of seeing Jesus in heaven in the hymns' final line. Jesus says to Bartimaeus in Mark 10: 'Go; your faith has made you well.' Bartimaeus then follows him. In order fully to encounter Jesus, perhaps we have to walk in God's fertile darkness, learning to trust and learning to have faith.

Prayer – read this through then close your eyes

God of living darkness come near us
God of the world's black depths enfold us
God of winter night time hold us
God of interstellar space be known to us
God of the depth of storm now speak to us
God of the empty tomb release us
Amen

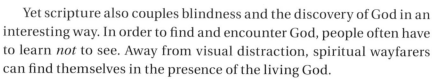

The double spiral: what do *others* look for?

We live in a visual culture. TV, cinema, advertising, magazines, computers, digital cameras, webcams, camera-phones, CCTV – everywhere there are visual images. It is unsurprising then, that when we investigate the spiritual journeys of people outside the mainstream religious traditions, we discover that what people see and how they themselves look is often an important part of their search for the divine.

Colours

Our culture spends a lot of time on ideas of beauty and what it is to be beautiful. Just as children are attracted by colour and quickly learn colour words to describe their world, so colour is increasingly important

in the lives of people on their spiritual journey. The rainbow colours, important to the New Age, have become for many filled with spiritual significance. For others, fractals, as discovered throughout the natural world, take on mystical significance, revealing complexity as they are enlarged. 🌐

Fractals: The Mandelbrot set

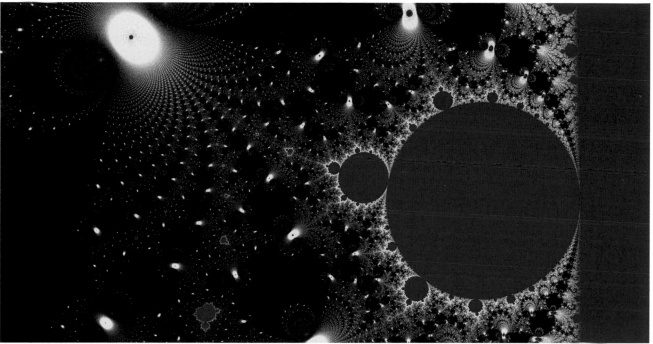

A woman was comforted at a funeral service when, waiting on a sunny day outside the crematorium, a sudden shower of rain threw up a double rainbow in the sky above. 'That's mum and dad. Well, I like to think so,' she said.

When Isaac Newton discovered that white light could be split into the rainbow by passing it through a prism, he discovered a secret that was locked up in 'ordinary' light, so many seekers today, recreating Newton's experiment are fascinated and moved by the rainbows emitted from crystals and prisms hung up in the sunlight. Seeing the sun, blue sky or the colours of nature also informs many people's spirituality and sense of God's presence, and Jesus himself exhorted his disciples to look at the lilies in the beauty in which God has created them.

Others try colour therapy, in which staring at or meditating on a particular hue or colour card is supposed to allow the energy of that colour to pass into the body and alter your emotional state.[6] You can build up a set of personal colour cards that are important to you. Similarly, aura therapy may involve a practitioner examining you to see what colour surrounds you and determine from that what treatment and healing you need to achieve a sense of well being and balance. You will also find that different colours are associated with emotions in books and on the internet, while others attribute different 'spiritual' colours to angels and other heavenly beings.[7]

Being beautiful

Many people also weave their spiritual search into the pursuit of personal beauty, so that they feel attractive and perceived as beautiful by others. It is a spirituality of finding themselves pleasing in the sight of all. What they see in the mirror becomes increasingly important. Colour is important here too. There is a make up programme called *Colour me Beautiful*, which has been used by the Revd Anne Hibbert, a Christian writer and speaker, to discuss how paying attention to our

outward appearance asks us to consider how beautiful we are on the inside. Both men and women may colour their hair, tint their eyelashes, whiten their teeth, have tattoos and pierce their bodies with coloured metal. Makeover programmes, in which ugly ducklings are turned into swans, houses and gardens transformed into havens of beautiful tranquillity, are very popular. Cosmetic surgery for both men and women becomes ever more fashionable. If you don't like the way God made you, you can change it. You have control over your looks and that control can be a part of your spiritual pilgrimage to find out who you really are. Feng Shui allows people to reorganise their homes so as to maximise the flow of 'good' energy and present a harmonised, visually pleasing environment in which to feel happy and peaceful.

In the same way, what they wear becomes part of people's spiritual identity as well as their fashion statement – and you can count on Trinny and Susanna to help you get it right. The connection between spirituality and fashion is seen in holistic lifestyle choices: goths make dramatic statements with black clothes accentuated with white; punks may dye their hair amazing colours and cut it into eye-catching shapes. But the pursuit of beauty may become an end in itself, so that the spiritual search becomes a means of fleeing from aging, from accepting our own imperfections, of despairing of finding a deep and meaningful loving relationship in which beauty is in the eye of the beholder. The spiritual journey of many people carries the whispered message *Keep young and beautiful if you want to be loved…* So what do people see when they see *us*? Here are some responses from Nick Spencer's research, *Beyond Belief.*

'If it's a lady [she'd be] sitting there with her cardie…And a long tent like skirts…a terrible paisley-patterned one!' (Female, 18–24, Nottingham);

'They try and be really quite cool, but they are not. They try a bit too hard!' (Female, 18–24, Nottingham);

and

'Fairly perfect…There's no earrings in noses…No body piercing.' (Mixed, 45–60, Nottingham).[8]

How would we *like* people to see us? And how does this relate to a theological understanding that we shall see God as he really is, with nothing hidden or concealed, 'face to face'?

Pursuing the beautiful

Another aspect of seeing in the spiritual journeys of people outside our tradition is the need to find icons and idols. In a visual culture, people can follow those who they feel have achieved the level of beauty and happiness they aspire to themselves. So people 'follow' Posh and Becks, or Brad and Angelina, or any of a whole host of celebrities and make them into their personal icons. Such celebrities themselves may display items of spiritual significance. For example, David Beckham wears cross necklaces and rosaries, and has a number of tattoos of winged angels and a winged cross on his body.[9] Magazines like *Hello* and *OK* encourage readers to look into the lives of others, enter their homes and find lifestyles and fashions to aspire to. People are encouraged to be voyeurs of lives not their own, a 'through the keyhole' experience in which to discover their own dreams and desires.

Abuse of seeing

The iGeneration Survey 2004 by Populus on behalf of *The Times*, a telephone poll of 1,004 18-to-30-year-olds, showed that 58% of those surveyed had looked at internet pornography. 'Pornography' covers a vast amount of visual material, but we have to acknowledge that images of violent physical and sexual abuse, including the exploitation and abuse of children are now, through the internet, much easier for people to obtain and use for their own interest, pleasure or gratification. In a visually oriented culture like ours, we are encouraged more and more to look at and watch all kinds of images and behaviour. Sometimes it is not a matter of choice, and images, ads and pop-ups can flash up on our screens that, all things being equal, we would rather not see. But in thinking about seeing, we have to be aware that there is visual material readily available to satisfy any temptation or desire. Gratifying such desire creates further demand which has to be filled. If we care about dignity and respect for other human beings under God, we have to be careful not to become part of the problem.

An important part of the journey into seeing within the double spiral of spirituality is learning to look away from what is readily offered to us, and to reject what is clearly not part of God's intention or desire. Images which show people using power to abuse others physically, mentally, sexually or emotionally must clearly be rejected. *But it is not enough to close our eyes and pretend that some of things we would rather not see are not there.* Sometimes we *have* to look, to be witnesses of atrocity, of abuse and injustice and to speak out against it. People can be changed by such witness, as the centurion saw in Jesus' agony the reality of his divine and human nature. Visual witness of atrocity can prompt others to action in order to transform God's broken world. We need to ask, *what is the result of my seeing this image?* We need careful discernment to know what kinds of seeing, watching and witness help others, and what kinds perpetuate abuse of power.

Watching and being watched

In George Orwell's classic novel, *1984*, human freedom and love were curtailed by constantly being watched by 'Big Brother'. In the film *Enemy of the State*, starring Will Smith and Gene Hackman, Smith's character discovers that he is being watched and manipulated by computers, satellites, and all kinds of hostile people that he never imagined could be there. We read in the newspapers about concerns about the limits on our freedom which various kinds of monitoring and watching bring. But Orwell's novel has sparked another phenomenon – reality TV and webcams where we can watch people all the time if we want to, including watching people being humiliated or manipulated. What does this explosion in watching people for entertainment purposes say about our use of the faculty of seeing?

Similarly, we have often held a comforting Christian view of God 'watching over us' as a parent does, making us feel loved and safe. But can we now understand those people outside the Church who find such a notion of a God watching over us – a 'Big Brother' God – both oppressive and unacceptable? What can we say to such people about the way God relates to the creation and to our lives?

The spirals entwined: walking with them

Our own spiritual journey involves learning to use the eyes God has given us and also learning to see clearly with the eyes of faith as we emerge from blindness and the dark mirror into the life that God holds out to us. Others too are using their eyes as they search and finding things which signify evidence of the divine. In what ways can we walk with such people and begin to find ways to share our faith and experiences? A good place to start the matter of reaching out to others through our visual media is to ask what we have already got that they would be interested in and want to know more about. If we do this, we will find that we already have rich resources in our churches and cathedrals, in our traditions of Christian art and in our worship.

Using our eyes, journeying into Christian tradition

The Christian Church has a long tradition of using visual images as a means of direct witness. In ancient churches, and in pre-literate communities, bible stories were often just painted on to the walls, so that people were reminded of the things Jesus did just by looking at the pictures around them. Many churches have stained glass windows which represent biblical scenes or lives of the saints, but how many people outside the Church now know enough background really to engage with the visual imagery we have inherited? How do we help people to use their eyes and to find out what a font is for, what the pulpit is for, why the altar has a cross on it, what a sanctuary lamp signifies? Do we even know what different visual emphases in other Christian denominations than our own tell us about the approach to God? How would you explain an Orthodox wedding ceremony to a non-Christian outsider? Can you explain a baptismal pool or the stations of the cross? Many people (apart from John Gray) enjoy wandering in a country churchyard, but how do ancient stones also speak of faith in a way that we can use as a means to witness to others? The truth is that, more often than not, we just don't use our eyes.[10]

Kitty, who cleans her local Catholic church every day, went to another denomination's chapel. Her reaction was: 'I don't know what they do in here – but it could do with a good clean.'

Take a look around

Go to your church, meeting place or place of fellowship or worship. What does it look like? Can you see, really see in your mind's eye, how the place where you worship and pray really appears, as a stranger would see it? What can you *see*? Furthermore, what does what you see *mean*?

Take the time to visit other churches in your area, especially those of other denominations.

❖ **Could you 'make sense' of this church for other people?**

❖ **What might you not be able to explain adequately?**

❖ **What would it take to find out?**

What is I.N.R.I.?

In James Joyce's *Ulysses*, Leopold Bloom wanders into a church and starts to wonder about what he sees. He wonders what the letters I.N.R.I. stand for and what I.H.S means. He decides that I.N R.I stands for 'Iron Nails Ran In' and I.H.S means 'I have suffered'.[11] If somebody asked you, would you be able to tell them what the letters *really* mean?

If a complete stranger, who knew nothing about the Christian faith whatsoever, wandered into your place of worship, how would that person know that Christians worship here? Would that person be able to find out something about Christian belief and practice? What could they find out from just using their eyes? It is interesting that many people have visited the 'virtual church' on the Internet. You can go in as a ghost and just explore the environment like you would in a computer game. Going in and having a look round does attract people. People often readily come to harvest and flower festivals because they enjoy the emphasis on beauty and the celebration of nature. They enjoy times when the church is decorated – at Christmas for example. The big churches, abbeys and cathedrals often have large visual displays for visitors which are extremely popular, especially with people who don't know where to start with such a visit. But what are they going to learn from your local situation? Who or what will be their guide?

What 'colour' is your church?

What will people see if they enter your church during worship? What would they see that would touch their own spiritual interests and journey? What could be done to create such bridges and connections?

Touching others through Christian art

The relationship between looking at visual things and the Christian faith has always been very strong. There is a tremendously long history of Christian art and it is interesting that the queues for the *Seeing Salvation* exhibition at the National Gallery in London often extended all round Trafalgar Square. To look upon and to meditate upon a great religious painting can really open up our understanding of our faith and reveal to us sides of, say, a biblical story that we had not previously thought about.

Similarly, the tradition of icons arose from an understanding that when we gaze upon an image, it can act as a window into God's own world. By learning to focus, reflect and immerse ourselves in prayer, we can use the visual image as a way of understanding God's heavenly kingdom and becoming convinced as well as immersed in its reality. ⊕

Christian visual art is still important and painters and sculptors are still finding inspiration and power in approaching the images of the Christian story. To do so, they often need to approach their own faith, or pray their works into being. One such young modern artist is Emma Kay. ⊕

Emma Kay: *Receiving Grace*

Using icons

Another important aspect of the tradition of Christian visual art is the use of icons to enable us to focus on God. The icon is much, much more than a painting; it is understood to be more like a window. As George Herbert says:

A man that looks on glass
On it may stay his eye
Or if he pleaseth, through it pass
And then the heaven espy.

So every icon is a way for us to focus our visual attention to enable prayer, and, through contemplation and prayer together, learn more of God and glimpse the heavenly reality. The Archbishop of Canterbury, Dr Rowan Williams, has written two books on icons which help us to understand the tradition and how to use icons as part of our spiritual journey.[12]

Looking at Icons

Give yourself at least five uninterrupted minutes to look at this famous icon.

❖ **What do you see?**

❖ **What other images and ideas came to mind?**

❖ **How might you use those images and ideas to form a prayer?**

❖ **How might you talk about this icon with someone who had no biblical background or knowledge of the Christian tradition?**

. . . .

A visual journey, the Stations (or the Way) of the Cross

In many churches and cathedrals it is possible to walk a journey around the building following Jesus' own last journey to crucifixion and enabling us to meditate on the events that happened after he was condemned to death. There are set prayers and liturgies for following this journey in the Christian tradition, but it is also possible to use the stations more informally as a way of focusing our personal thoughts and feelings about the way Jesus died for us. Religious communities often have the stations as part of a prayer garden, so that people can combine the natural idea of 'going for a walk' with opportunities for prayer. While in many cathedrals, the stations are works of art by famous artists, it is also possible for them to be made by the local community or by children, perhaps for use during Lent or in Holy Week. Some churches have used tapestry, painted cloth, children's drawings or reclaimed rubbish to make the stations.[13] The stations also do not have to be fixed, but can be used creatively as a visual journey anywhere and can be helpful in teaching people who have no Christian background about what happened to Jesus and what God did in him, for all of us.

Colours, images, nature

Leafy-with-love-banks and
the green waters of the canal

Pouring redemption
for me, that I do

The will of God, wallow in
the habitual, the banal,

Grow with nature again
as before I grew.

Patrick Kavanagh, *Canal Bank Walk*

One of the ways in which we can come close to others in the double spiral of spiritual journeys is by using the methods of Ignatian spirituality[14] to reach out and find points of contact. Ignatian spirituality encourages us to find God in all things, to look for God in the natural world and to make spaces for creative and unfettered reflection. We are asked to reflect on our experiences and make sense of the things that happen to us so that we can better discern God at work in our lives and in the lives of others. The spiral journey we have been following in mission is characterised in Ignatius' teaching by gratitude to God, by service to others, by recognising God's help and by trying to discern God's will.

Exploring your community

Take time to walk around a local park or other open space. Is God here? What are other people doing here? What can you see that can feed the spiritual journey?

Take time to walk around a shopping centre. Is God here? What are other people doing here? What can you see that can feed the spiritual journey?

Reflect on your experiences. Write down what you saw and what you saw people doing. How can we connect with these lives?

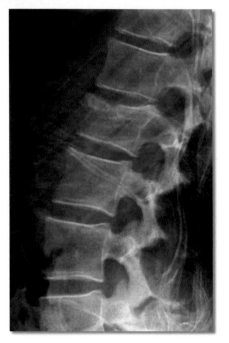

Where have we been?

This chapter has asked us to reflect on what it is to have been given eyes and the gift of sight.

❖ How are we supposed to use our eyes to see and understand? We need to realise that our range of vision is limited although we can explore the complexity of the world through our technology and our imagination. There are other ways of seeing what cannot be perceived directly.

❖ How can we learn to see and recognise God? Our spiritual journey requires us to employ the eyes of faith to see God at work and to join in with what God is asking of us. But we need to pay attention or we can miss what God is doing.

❖ What does it mean to be blind? What can we learn about our own faith from those who have no physical sight? What are the limitations of being sighted? God is God of dark as well as light. In the dark places of the world, God is there. How will we know his presence?

❖ Others outside the Church are also using their eyes. Our culture and society stresses the importance of making sure that what we see is pleasing to us. How does this affect the spiritual journey and how are we too seduced by this?

❖ How can the act of seeing be abused? How does using our eyes exploit and victimise others? When are we part of the problem? What is the place of witness and testimony to the abuse we see in the world?

❖ What does our church look like to non-Christians? How can they make sense of what it contains and what is done there? What connections are possible? What visual resources have we got and how can they be used to full advantage to speak into people's spiritual journeys of faith in Christ?

❖ Reflection on our church resources also requires that we pay more attention to God's work in the world. We need to pray and reflect on what we see and discern the opportunities for sharing faith that God lays before us.

Meditate on Psalm 121:1

I lift up my eyes to the hills –
From where will my help come?
My help comes from the Lord
Who made heaven and earth.

Journey into Hearing

Inside, hollowness; what is
comes to me as a blow, but not
a wound

Archbishop Rowan Williams

Starting the journey: what is hearing?

Like seeing, hearing is fundamentally important to the way we experience the world around us. If we live in a visual culture, we also live in an aural culture. Our 'shell-like' ears are remarkable organs capable of collecting all kinds of sounds and vibrations and conveying them via delicate membranes, bones and chambers to our brains. Through hearing we discern the complexity of God's creation: we learn the sounds and rhythms of wind and rain, the sounds of leaves rustling, waves on the shore, the calls of birds and animals. We learn the sounds of human living, the noise of aircraft and traffic, the ringing of phones and cash tills, the clatter of computer keyboards and the bustle of kitchens and factories. As human beings we seek out pleasurable sounds, turn away from unpleasant sounds and react instinctively to other kinds of sounds. If we hear laughter, we may begin to laugh too. If someone cries, we may become upset and wish to offer comfort. At the cinema, the soundtrack can make all the difference to the scary suspense or emotional content of a film. Ask people to describe the film *Jaws* and they are more than likely to imitate the famous 'shark approach' music. The intensity of the film *Brief Encounter*, derives mainly from the use of Rachmaninov's music as a powerfully emotional musical background. We respond especially to singing – and singing has always been a response to human emotion and a symbol of the human spirit. We may 'sing for joy' or use singing to protest or to lament or mourn. Hostages and prisoners abused by their captors have been known to defy them by singing. As humans we have an ability to hear ranges from very high pitched sounds to low rumbles, but some animals can detect sounds outside our own range – your dog, but not you, can hear a dog-whistle. Prey animals may have particularly acute hearing and very mobile ears that will help them realise a predator is on the prowl. Yet even within the limits of our own hearing there is a tremendous variety of extraordinary sound.

Listening

There is so much sound to hear, indeed, that like most mammals, we have developed the important facility of *listening*, of devoting attention to particular sounds and filtering out the background noise. The extraordinary ability to concentrate on one stream of sound, to 'tune in', is critical to our lives as social and family creatures and it is especially important to us as spiritual beings. As human beings, we have developed a unique ability to communicate at a level of sophistication far beyond the other living creatures with whom we share our planet: we alone have a complex of detailed and intricate languages. To communicate effectively with one another, the process of hearing and listening becomes especially important. It is often said that our hearing is 'the last thing to go' and that talking to someone even in deep coma, may be important to provoke response and the way back to healing. The act of listening penetrates deep into our imaginations and stirs our thoughts – which is why radio continues to be such a powerful medium.

Attention

What is it about us that allows us to concentrate on one conversation at a party, or to realise that our mobile phone is ringing deep in a pocket?

What is it about the way we hear that allows us to get tunes or advertising jingles stuck in our heads, or recognise a beloved voice on a crackly phone line? We may listen out for certain sounds – a clock chiming the hour, the cot rattling, the turn of a key in the lock, the phone ringing, the microwave's ping, the rumble of thunder, our own child's voice in the crowd at the school gate? Some sounds may become extremely important to us, and reinforce the idea that we love and are loved. Bereaved people often report hearing familiar noises made by loved ones, even though they have died. Speaking and listening go together and become the glue of relationships, the way we form community. Because of this, hearing, attention and what we choose to listen to has a profound role to play in our spiritual journeys. Simone Weil says 'absolutely unmixed attention is prayer'. David Hay reminds us that this allows us to connect with others in an important way:

> **Our role is to be listeners, with no purpose other than trying to understand what people are saying to us when they talk about their spirituality. This 'sounding board' approach seems to give powerful permission for people to speak about existential issues that are normally obscured in everyday life.**[1]

One of the problems Christians have is that we often fail to hear things in a certain way. We *assume* that what we hear fits a particular picture of the world, but fail to understand what we hear as a way in which God is capable of transforming the world. Suppose that sounds are creatures, each coming to us with its own message of what God is doing – what then, would we *really* hear?

Stop and Listen

Stop what you are doing for ten minutes. Make a list of everything you can hear, how many different sounds, both those exterior to you and the sounds of your body. Become aware of how much sound you have access to. Are the sounds pleasing or unpleasant? Is there something in particular you are listening out for?

Moving out: hearing God in our time

There are two particular aspects of hearing and sound that we can concentrate on as we move out in our spiral journey to hear God in the world around us: music and the spoken word. Both are particularly significant in hearing God in our time.

Worship

By an Act of understanding therefore be present now with all the creatures among which you live; and hear them in their beings and operations praising God in an heavenly manner. Some of them vocally, others in their ministry, all of them naturally and continually. We infinitely wrong ourselves by laziness and confinement. All creatures in all nations, and tongues and people praise God infinitely; and the more, for being your sole and perfect treasures. You are never what you ought till you go out of yourself and walk among them.

Thomas Traherne *Centuries* II–78.

'And suddenly there was
with the angel a multitude
of the heavenly host,
praising God and saying,
*"Glory to God in the
highest heaven,
and on earth peace among
those whom he favours!"'*
Luke 2:13–14

In *The Silmarillion,*
JRR Tolkien imagines
a cosmology based on
perfect harmony (goodness,
rightness) interrupted by
discord, dissonance (evil), in
his constructed mythology
behind *The Lord of the Rings.*

Scripture tells us that we are made for worship and that worship is typically characterised by the sound we make and sound we hear. In glimpses of heaven, made accessible to human beings, prayer, praise, exaltation, singing and making music are the means by which humans know they are in the presence of the transcendent. In the Psalms for instance, each psalm is a sound-world in itself, lifting the earth up into God's presence for God to change according to his will. But does our worship measure up to that, or is the music or prayer just a filler for the rest of the service? Historically, in the layout of cathedrals and large churches, the choir is situated before the altar to give worshippers coming up to the altar a foretaste of heaven. There is great concentration on the beauty of worship as an aural experience in the free churches too.

At Pentecost, the coming of the Holy Spirit is signalled by an outburst of sound, with a tremendous variety of speaking and listening, so that everyone within reach is touched by God's word to them in their own language, intimate and real. So it is that in some Christian traditions, the sense of the Holy Spirit being among a community, or the overwhelming sense of the transcendent reality of the moment is characterised by speaking or singing 'in tongues', by glossolalia, an outpouring of sound.

The Word in creation

Thou whose almighty Word
Chaos and darkness heard
And took their flight

Scripture tells us also that hearing God, being in communication with God, is a fundamental part of the created order. At the creation, all this comes into being by the command of God's eternal Word, uttered and made real. So St John tells us:

In the beginning was the Word
And the Word was with God
And the Word was God
John 1:1

The *logos* of God is much more than speech, it is bound up with the act of creating and becoming. Jesus is this Word made flesh and dwelling among us. Throughout his ministry Jesus stresses the importance of listening to God's word and paying proper *spiritual* attention to it. The way we pay attention to God both equips and changes us in the ways necessary to spread the word to others. The idea of *logos* tells us that the way we ourselves hear, communicate and respond is itself intimately related to constructing the world and making new things happen in the world. This is interesting, because in ancient thought, people such as Pythagoras imagined that the universe was built upon musical principles of perfect sound and today cosmic string theories suggest that the tiniest elements of the quantum universe may be like resonating strings giving rise to the physics we encounter. Our own ability to respond to vibration and sound waves in the form of hearing therefore may intersect the world as God creates and sustains it. Through our technology we can hear the eternal whispered sounds

In Corinthians 1:13 St Paul talks about his witness as a form of dissonance, 'a clanging cymbal' if it is not characterised by love.

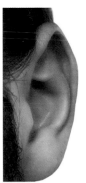

of the beginning of the universe. We can indeed encounter the music of the spheres.

When we speak of God, when we pray and praise, we are participating in the creative activity God sustains in the world. Thus, in our proclamation, in whatever form that might take, we have a tremendous responsibility to take all our spoken and sung witness, prayer and worship seriously. In scripture, for example, blessing and cursing were powerful acts which effected change in the community, as we see in Isaac's blessing in Genesis 27:28–9. For example,

> *The Lord spoke to Moses, saying: Speak to Aaron and his sons, saying. Thus you shall bless the Israelites: You shall say to them,*
>
> *The Lord bless you and keep you;*
> *The Lord make his face to shine upon you, and be gracious to you;*
> *The Lord lift up his countenance upon you, and give you peace.*
>
> *So shall they put my name on the Israelites, and I will bless them.*
> Numbers 6:22–7

As we move out on the spiral path of our spiritual journey, we need to be aware of the power of words to bless and to hurt others, to hurt ourselves and to cause so much damage.

Think about blessing and cursing

Can you think of a time when you said something hurtful you didn't mean or someone said something hurtful to you? What does it mean to curse someone?[1] Why do the words hurt so badly?

Can you think of a time when you said something to make people feel better about themselves or made people feel praised or loved? What was their reaction? How do you feel when people express joy, love or blessing towards you? When might people bless or curse God?

In the film *8 Mile*, starring the rap artist Eminem and based on his life, there is a ritual form of cursing, 'cussing', employed by the young poor people as a means of using language to protest at and escape from a world that doesn't care about them.

Spend time with this prayer based on Corinthians 4:2–6

Lord, open to us a door for the word,
That we may declare the mystery of Christ.
May we declare it clearly, as we should.
May we act wisely towards others,
Making the most of time spent with them.
May our speech always be gracious and courteous.
May our speech be seasoned with salt,
With a proper spiritual understanding.
May we know the right thing to say
To allow them to hear not us, but you.
Amen

God speaks to us

Much of our scriptural language about relationship with God is given to us as forms of hearing and response. It is also important that the way God speaks is personal and comes to us in our 'own' language. We may ourselves be so used to hearing about God in English that we don't think there is anything odd about it, but the experience of the Bible Society can shake us out of this complacency.

Weeka Musuku from the former Zaire, explains why this is so special: 'Now we have the Bible in Ngbaka, God speaks clearly and directly to our hearts! It is like Christ has come to visit us.'[2]

The challenge of the way God speaks to us also affects what we hear when we preach in Church. Are people searching along their own spiritual journey able to make sense of what they hear and find it resonating with their own lives?

God's call

God calls people. They hear him and respond to him and powerful relationships are formed which determine the course of the spiritual journeys for whole peoples.

O let me hear thee speaking
In accents clear and still;
Above the storms of passion
The murmurs of self will

Then the Lord came and stood there calling as before 'Samuel! Samuel!'
and Samuel said 'Speak, for your servant is listening'

1 Samuel 3:10

Similarly, Jesus calls people to follow him and they leave what they are doing and become his disciples. Here is a connection between Christian vocation ('calling') and the spiral journey out into God's world. When Jesus calls us and we respond, it changes the path we are making for ourselves.

Listening to Jesus

As Jesus passed along the Sea of Galilee, he saw Simon and his brother Andrew casting a net into the sea – for they were fishermen. And Jesus said to them, 'Follow me and I will make you fishers for people.' And immediately they left their nets and followed him. As he went a little farther, he saw James, son of Zebedee and his brother John, who were in their boat mending the nets. Immediately he called them; and they left their father Zebedee in the boat with the hired men, and followed him.

Mark 1:16–20.

The Christian life is guided by careful listening for and responding to a call that is made by God to each of us both personally and in community. That call to discipleship, to follow Christ and be obedient to God's will, involves a particular kind of attention. And although we may spend plenty of time being attentive to God in church, how often do we listen for the divine word in our daily lives and in the speech of others and in the sounds of our world? The disciples were after all going about their work and their daily tasks when Jesus spoke to them.

Read and reflect on this story

A woman was phoned by a hospice to say that her mother was dying. In a panic, she got in her car and raced to the hospice, but every little thing seemed to slow her down. After a while, she felt instinctively that her mother had already died and she began to cry. Blinded by tears, she said aloud 'why am I doing this?' Immediately she heard a voice say very clearly 'because we love her'. The shock of this made the woman stop the car and stop crying and try to understand what she had just heard. It seemed to her that God was identifying with her distress and reminding her it did not matter if she was not present at the moment of death because God's love was with her mother even if she was not. Her mother knew she was loved. Later, it also occurred to the woman that if she had not stopped to think about the mysterious voice, she might have had an accident.

- ❖ Have you ever had an experience when you thought God spoke to you in some way?
- ❖ How might such an experience connect with the experiences of others outside the Church?

God hears our prayers

Lord, hear us
Lord, graciously hear us

We typically ask God to 'hear' our prayers and imagine prayer as a form of communication which goes from our mouths to God's ears. There is therefore a particular power to spoken or sung prayer made in community, going out from us towards God.

Moreover, we may not realise it but the fact that we pray connects us with the spirituality of very many people outside the Church – and people also believe that God does respond to their prayers:

In great unhappiness or fear many people, including those who are uncertain about God's existence, turn to prayer for help. A total of 37% of those recently questioned [in the Soul of Britain survey] feel they have received such help – a 40% increase on 1987.[3]

Many Christians report that they encounter people who are looking for active help to find out how to pray and how to receive confidence that God both hears and responds to prayer.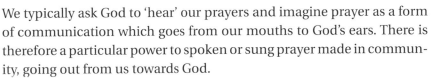

Reflect on the meaning of prayer

When you are praying, do not heap up empty phrases as the Gentiles do; for they think that they will be heard because of their many words.

Matthew 6:7

And prayer is more
Than an order of words, the conscious occupation
Of the praying mind, or the sound of the voice praying

T S Eliot, *Little Gidding*[4]

? If someone said 'teach me how to pray', how would you respond?

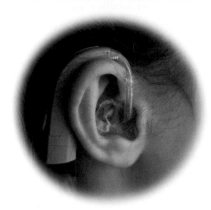

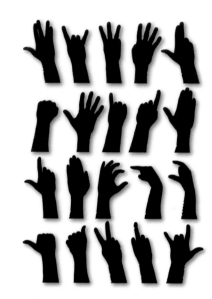

Journey beyond hearing: being deaf

Many of us will as we age, become hard of hearing and perhaps have more difficulty in paying attention to the sounds we want to concentrate on. If we have started out as hearing people, used to the rich language of hearing and communication that we have in scripture and in prayer and worship, we may experience a sense of loss and deprivation.

But people who have been born deaf or who become 'totally' deaf quite early on may have surprising things to teach us about the world they inhabit. The percussionist Evelyn Glennie is one such person who can amaze us with her skill with her instruments, although she does not experience sound as hearing people do.[5] She says:

How then do the terms 'disabled' or 'Deaf' really apply to me? In short, they don't, not even the 'Hearing Impaired' label works because in some respects my hearing is superior to the average non-impaired person.[6]

So those with musical ability often have access to more finely textured hearing environments. We could argue that we too should have our ears attuned more closely to what God is saying to us? How then do we allow the Holy Spirit to tutor and nurture that ability in us? Or do we simply continue on our way with 'deaf ears'?

The world of the deaf is one of intense communication and variety and one in which the facility of *attention* is developed to its highest level. Deaf people who learn sign language or who learn to lip read cannot afford our lazy ways. Deaf people must pay close attention to how we move and sign, the world of communication takes place in a shared space between the people signing, a space filled with drama, movement, humour and emotion. For this reason, deaf people are particularly adept at worship, in opening and describing the space in which God and human beings can come together and know one another. There are therefore deaf churches and deaf choirs.

Many deaf people therefore feel that it is our typical hearing community that is in deficit because we do not have access to their richly textured culture. This young person describes it to us:

I have not gold
I have the richness of faith in the fold
I have not hate
I have thousands of peers with which to relate
I have not a mansion
I have only great passion
I have not a treasure
I have hope that one cannot measure
I have not fear
I have in my heart life which is dear
I have not hearing
I have the favor of caring.

Rich, aged 16[7]

Hearing-people learning to sign often find it difficult to enter the world of the deaf, but one way in which thinking about the journey beyond hearing can focus our attention is to consider the importance and function of silence in our relationship with God.

Silence and 'deafness'

Human beings in today's society often long for 'peace and quiet' but have trouble with silence. Many people live with the television constantly murmuring in the background or surrounded by some other form of noise. Children often like to do their homework with earphones feeding them their favourite music. We see people with mobile phones clamped to their ears; it is known that some people even talk into their mobiles when there is no one on the other end, telling the story of themselves to others around. This is the iPod generation, where the familiar white earphones indicate that you have your entire music collection with you at all times. In scripture there is much metaphor about the word of God falling on 'deaf ears' as the parable of the sower makes clear (Matthew 13 cf Isaiah 6), but it is not physical deafness that is the problem, but a spiritual deafness in which we are distracted from the possibility of hearing what God has to say to us. How then, do we use silence creatively on our own spiritual journey and enable others to unstop their ears, deafened by distraction?

The Quaker tradition has always used silence in worship, leaving it up to individual members to break it only as the Spirit leads. There is no pressure to 'perform' or to fill up time with words. Silence is a form of permission-giving for each person to focus on their own and others' spiritual needs and to experience more clearly what God is saying about the broken world. In silence, attention can be brought to bear on what God is saying. However, in much Christian prayer and worship today, times of silence end up only being perfunctory, a mere gap between different elements of the liturgy. What does it take to make silence 'work' in our spiritual journey?

The Dominican religious order has this to tell us about the importance of silence as a preparation for sharing our faith:

> **Silence prepares our bodies, our minds, our hearts and our spirit for prayer and study. A rich, pregnant silence enables us to hand ourselves over to God, to become more conscious of our own woundedness, and to see, listen, and respond to the risen Christ in our brothers and sisters. Finally, silence propels us to go out and preach.**[8]

We should also be aware that in a world dominated by noise, more and more people from outside the Church are looking for places, such as religious community retreat houses, where they can be silent for a while. How can we help people to find the silence they need?

Where do you go to be silent? How important is silence to you on your spiritual journey?

The double spiral: what do others hear?

Going out

Music plays an increasingly large part in people's lives, and many young people like to listen to pop music or go clubbing to meet friends, dance and party. Consequently different genres of modern music often form an important part of people's spiritual journeys. The group *Faithless* sang that the dancefloor was the 'church' for the clubber, where all hurts could be healed and the DJ was God and the artist *P!nk*, takes up this theme:

> *If God is a DJ*
> *Life is a dance floor*
> *Love is the rhythm*
> *You are the music*
> *If God is a DJ*
> *Life is a dance floor*
> *You get what you're given*
> *It's all how you use it* [9]

Different music genres have different kinds of spiritual outlook and understanding. Euphoric trance may concentrate on the idea of a loved-up heavenly bliss invoked by the music and club atmosphere: 'Happiness happening'. This is a long way from the powerful angry rhythms of *Hatebreed* or *Rammstein* articulating the sense of disturbance, anger and anxiety about a broken world. The urban sound is different again from 'pure' R&B or soul genres. In some forms of modern music, especially rap, the lyric is all-important, in dance music, it is the remixed rhythms and melodies which drive the experience of the track. What do we, as Christians, have to say within this varied music culture?

Many pop musicians use faith concepts, either implicitly or explicitly stated. This is clear just from just looking at mainstream pop bands. *The Manic Street Preachers* for example have released albums called *Gold against the Soul* (1993), *The Holy Bible* 1994 (re-released 2004) and *This is my truth, tell me yours* (1998). Robbie Williams, apart from releasing one of the most played and covered contemporary songs, *Angels*, also includes faith imagery and religious questioning in his lyrics. Other bands invoke images of spiritual warfare between good and evil, God and the Devil. To make connections between our 'Christian' language and the languages of the world of contemporary music, we have to find out what the music is saying to people. What are we to make of someone whose spiritual life is girded up by listening to a Goth group such as H.I.M.? This group uses images of hell and damnation to symbolise the pain of relationships with the hope of somehow being able to vanquish the darkness and find a true and everlasting love. Song titles include: 'Buried alive by love', 'the Funeral of hearts' 'Beyond redemption', 'Soul on Fire', 'The Sacrament' and 'Endless dark'. 🌐

**i was raised in the womb
groomed by christ
with a gift to raise souls
from the tomb
Please don't assume
we aint tryna take the spot
blow the plot
worldwide still parta the plot**

Grits, Here We Go, 2002

One of the challenges to us is to understand how this music connects with people's spiritual search, but we also to ask ourselves 'what do people hear when they listen to us?'

One of the problems is perhaps that mainstream bands exploring faith issues touch the Christian tradition only tangentially, and while there are explicitly Christian bands such as *Delirious?*,[9] such bands often tend to end up in a niche – as just another specialist genre. Christian rock often apes the genre, it doesn't enter the darkness or go through the angst. Another problem is that the Christian environment surrounding some very successful singers, such as Britney Spears or Beyoncé, ends up being exploited or discarded as fame takes a hold. What people hear when they encounter such artists does not help them make sense of Christian commitment. What we do need to look out for and to be aware of is bands and artists negotiating the cross-over between genre music and those artists exploring their faith. One example is the group Grits.

Bonafide and Coffee, the *Grits* duo, present us with a challenge about how we hear Christian music, when they say: 'In the Christian music industry, everything's predominantly white. Black music doesn't really exist in that genre....When you look at Jesus, he went out and ministered in cultures where people didn't even think he should be. "Sir, why are you talking to me? You shouldn't even be talking to me," said the woman at the well. His example of breaking those boundaries is what we're trying to follow.'[10] Are we guilty of sanitising music for our own use so that our own Christian microculture is disconnected from reality? In the history of church music, we realise that West End gallery bands and other forms of popular music were pushed out of church by the clericalism of robed choirs and organ music, which are now 'identified' with the church musical tradition.

Consequently, when people come to us for the occasional offices, they can often be presented with books full of lovely hymns, but find nothing that speaks to their spiritual journey. Further, in an attempt to provide more modern music, some expressions of worship make do with material that is at worst sentimental, derivative and cloying. Some lyrics are unbiblical and even heretical.

Chilling out

On their spiritual journeys, people outside the Church often surround themselves with sounds that help to turn their minds away from the stress of modern living – 'chill-out' music. Spiritually nourishing music can take the form of natural sounds, ocean music, whale songs, music based on the rhythms and sounds found in nature. Equally, people may turn to the classical tradition of music composed in the worship of God, so that you can purchase 'Chill Out Classics' such as selected pieces of Bach, Mozart or Vivaldi. Yet Robin Leaver reminds us that:

'Bach's music will never be understood if it is only heard out of context in a concert hall. It was not composed to be merely listened to. It was written to be participated in as a part of the worship of the Christian church. It was written for the ministry of the Word, sharing the proclamation of the Christian gospel with the lections and the sermon.'[11]

Similarly, people outside the Church may take and adapt Christian music, such as Gregorian chant. Some music released commercially by religious communities have become enormously popular as a way of relaxing after a long day at work and make unusual celebrities of people for whom such prayer and music is simply part of a daily life lived before God. The challenge to us is to recognise the profound spiritual need implied by 'chill-out' music and to build new connections between the music that meets that need and the worship of almighty God.

Think about your musical tastes

What is your favourite 'chill-out' music?
Why is it important to you?

Abusive noise

In his book *An Evil Cradling* Brian Keenan reports that one of the worst things his captors did to him was to hang a radio tuned to nothing but static turned up to full volume and blasting into his cell day and night. Unable to turn it off or filter it out, he became ill and unable to hear. People afflicted with tinnitus (ringing in the ears) or other dysfunctions of hearing often say that they are being driven mad by the inability to focus attention or to find places of quiet. Some people with psychiatric disease are plagued by loud and unpleasant noises or voices in their heads.

Noise can be a particular source of unhappiness or discord. Noisy neighbours, screaming and shouting or playing loud music can be a misery. Parents can be driven to distraction by incessantly crying babies or whining children and some children have been hurt because adults lash out when they feel they can't stand the incessant noise any longer. Many people are irritated by having to sit next to somebody on a long journey whose music is erupting from their headphones, or listening to somebody rustle sweet papers in the cinema. Others' lives are made difficult by traffic, pneumatic drills or aircraft noise. In some areas, noise pollution is a serious problem, disrupting people's daily lives. Being subjected to loud noise or cacophonous music when you are ill can intensify the sense of suffering.

There can be problems with perceptions of 'abusive' noise in church. Some people find the noises babies and small children make unbearable and then insist that the children are taken out. Others react to the type of music. Others can be dreadfully disturbed during prayer by people chattering, laughing or even shouting. Cathedral worship can be troubled by the movements of visitors and the clicking of camera shutters. Sometimes open doors of welcome are shut because of nuisance from traffic. But if non-church-goers come to the church, will they also find themselves faced with abusive noise, the spiritual equivalent of static?

Think about unpleasant noise

What kinds of noise drive you mad? Why?

Are there certain sorts of noises which either cause disturbance or which are not 'allowed' in your church?

Use the internet and go to church

Look at the 'Mystery Worshipper' section of the Ship of Fools website http://ship-of-fools.com/Mystery. Use the formula in that section to listen carefully to a typical service at your own church. If possible take a non-church-goer with you to do the same thing. How did your church come out?

The Spirals entwined, walking with them

There are various ways in which our own Christian hearing journey and that of others outside the Church become entwined.

Music

We have to be aware what people hear from us when they come into the Church's life. When people come for the odd service, or for the occasional offices, what are they looking for, what are they waiting to hear? Although regular churchgoing as a tradition has changed its patterns, many people still have a favourite hymn that stays with them from school or from going to weddings or baptisms. Is it possible to explore what it means to them? Hymns have passed into different parts of our culture, so that *Abide with Me* is sung at football matches and *Swing Low Sweet Chariot* at rugby fixtures. Hymn-singing has also been a means of protest, the articulation of the dream of transformation which we can see in music from black gospel, American and African spirituals, to Greenham Common. When people feel deeply about what it means to be human and the relationship of human beings to our world, they often turn to religious music. Carols are still a particular Christmas favourite in the life of people outside the Church and many carols, like traditional folksongs, approach Christian life in a robust, even violent way, which resonates with people's experience.[12]

But what happens when people request us for other kinds of music, outside the Christian tradition? Where might we want to draw the line, and why? We need to understand more fully what kinds of music people listen to and seek to understand what that contributes to their spiritual growth.

Prayer

In responding to people's spiritual needs, one of the things we could realise is that almost any of the sounds going on around us can become the focus for a person to begin to pray.

Put together, we can understand how quiet meditative prayer through music has a special appeal, as in Taizé worship and the meditative worship songs of Iona.

Reflect on *Prayer* by Carol Ann Duffy

Some days, although we cannot pray, a prayer
utters itself. So, a woman will lift
her head from the sieve of her hands and stare
at the minims sung by a tree, a sudden gift.

Some nights, although we are faithless, the truth
enters our hearts, that small familiar pain;
then a man will stand stock-still, hearing his youth
in the distant Latin chanting of a train.

Pray for us now. Grade I piano scales
console the lodger looking out across
a Midlands town. Then dusk, and someone calls
a child's name as though they named their loss.

Darkness outside. Inside, the radio's prayer –
Rockall. Malin. Dogger. Finisterre.[13]

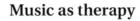

? **What everyday sounds stir your memories and link to your spiritual journey?**

Music as therapy

Music can also be used to help people in specific ways. For example, music can provide a context for dealing with painful emotions and memories. It can help people who are disorganised, by providing structure and a way to measure time. It can stimulate memory and for some people, motivate them into completing tasks and assignments. The poet Christopher Smart (1722–71) who suffered from insanity wrote movingly of the power of music to order his chaotic thoughts 'when I am reminded by the instruments' and he sees music as the bringer of God's kingdom of heaven:

For the trumpet of God is a blessed intelligence
And so are all the instruments in Heav'n.
For God the Father Almighty plays upon the harp
Of stupendous magnitude and melody.
For at that time malignity ceases
And the devils themselves are at peace.
For this time is perceptible to man
By a remarkable stillness and serenity of soul.

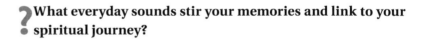

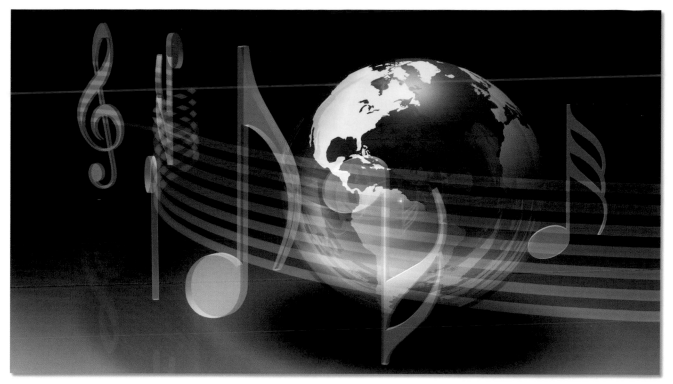

Pure music without words can be less threatening for anxious or hurt people. There are also many ways to participate in music which can be affirming for people who have low self-esteem. Because of this potential of music as a therapeutic agent, we should also not forget that our own music traditions can be of benefit in nurturing spirituality and in bringing healing to hurt.

Using our ears, journeying into Christian tradition

There is still a tremendous interest in traditional religious music as is evidenced by the sales of artists such as Aled Jones, Charlotte Church, and Haley Westenra. Classic FM also regularly plays requests for church music favourites like *Ave Maria* and *O for the Wings of a Dove*. Music remains a powerful emotive force for many people's spiritual lives and even people unfamiliar with the tradition can be inspired by the high standards of organ music and cathedral music that we have in our country.

Beverly Knight MBE, is a sucessful British soul singer who also hosts the Radio 2 show *Beverley's Gospel Nights* exploring the origins and impact of gospel music, which even features in performances by superstars like Elton John.

But do we ever stop long enough to think what a powerful evangelistic witness making music and singing can be to people outside the Church? For some people travelling to the Christmas festivities in the Bluewater shopping centre, the greatest source of delight is not the illuminated reindeer or the decorated shops, but the Salvation Army band playing Christmas music. Some Christian traditions spend a great deal of time on the preparation and delivery of music in praise of God and the traditions of eg Gospel music have translated into the modern pop culture that so many people enjoy. Yet there are so many Christian churches where people don't want to sing or find it difficult to do so. And we know that the music in worship can be a sticking point for many. But it is worth thinking about this in terms of mission. If strangers were standing at the church door listening, would the sound of Christians worshipping together inspire them to think more of God, or urge them to come in?

Where have we been?

This chapter has asked us to consider what is like to have ears and enjoy the gift of hearing.

❖ What does it mean to be able to hear? How many different kinds of sound are there in the world? What is the difference between hearing and listening? What does it mean to pay attention to sounds, music, voices? Can we learn to hear God in *all* the sounds we encounter?

❖ We understand different kinds of sound to be associated with God. We learn of worship through music, praise, prayer and thanksgiving. The Pentecost experience shows that exalted praise is not just the privilege of heaven, but can inspire us too. We also have the tradition of Jesus as the Father's creative Word made flesh, so that through our ability to make sounds and music, we participate in the creative process. Because we can both bless and curse, we must take our sound-making seriously.

❖ Through scripture we learn that God speaks to us and calls us. This can be a powerful experience when we encounter this speaking in our own language as an intimate and personal event. People inside and outside the Church are still experiencing this personal call today.

❖ Many people believe God hears and responds to prayer, but outside the Christian tradition it may be difficult for people to decide how to pray. In order to connect with them, we first have to make sense of our own prayer life and traditions.

❖ Those who cannot hear as we do may have much to tell us about the spiritual encounter and about worship, if only we have 'ears to hear'. Jesus warns us about not listening and the need to pay careful attention to what we hear. We need to think about the importance of silence as a place for spirituality to be nurtured and to grow.

❖ Music is espccially important in today's society as a means of enjoyment and of relaxing. Within the many different types of music people follow there are many musicians and bands articulating the spiritual search. Do we pay any attention to the spiritual aspects of this music and know how to respond to it?

❖ We need to be aware of abusive noise. Are we ever guilty of interrupting others' worship through thoughtless noise?

❖ We need to think carefully about the way people approach us with stories of the music of their spiritual journey. Are we willing to accommodate them? We need to help them find meaningful music, not as wallpaper for services, but as something which expresses their journey. Similarly, we need to find the connections which give people tools for rich and meaningful prayer.

❖ The Christian tradition contains music capable of displaying God's creative and redemptive action in the world and this musical tradition is entrusted to us. What do we have to do to be worthy of it and recognise its evangelistic potential?

Reflect on Psalm 67: a song

To the leader: with stringed instruments.

May God be gracious to us and bless us
And make his face to shine upon us, *Selah*
That your way may be known upon earth,
Your saving power among the nations.
Let the peoples praise you, O God;
Let all the peoples praise you.

Let the nations be glad and sing for joy,
For you judge the peoples with equity
And guide the nations upon the earth. *Selah*
Let the peoples praise you O God;
Let all the peoples praise you.

The earth has yielded its increase;
God, our God has blessed us.
May God continue to bless us;
Let all the ends of the earth revere him.

Not only servicing the lungs, the air
is woven, full
of needles.

Archbishop Rowan Williams

Journey into Smell

Starting the journey: what is smell?

'I smell, therefore I am'

When we breathe in, the air we pass through the receptors in our noses comes full of information about the world around us. Smells are literally everywhere. Like all gaseous substances, they expand to fill the space available to them: once released from an aerosol, a liquid fragrance will evaporate and then dissipate. 'Making sense' – of things and of people – really can be expressed as 'making scents'. The ability to smell is the one sense that connects more of ourselves with more of the world; smell continues to inform us even when our other senses can tell us little or nothing.

The ability to smell also confirms for us an intrinsic part of who we are, for we all have our own distinctive fragrance that subliminally identifies us to those whom we know and love. But our personal fragrance goes much deeper than that. We each have a smell that can only be masked, not eradicated cosmetically. At this level, our smell connects us with our loved ones, indeed our personal pheromones are apparently the basis of sexual attraction – which in this sense is quite literally 'personal chemistry'. To lose one's smell is to lose one's identity. Smells welcome us home, warn us of danger, and form some of the most powerful bonds between human beings. They evoke memories of times, places and experiences.

The smell of familiar places can be reassuring: we all know what home smells like, and if another person's home has smells that are radically different from our own we can feel uncomfortable in it. Too many smells can have the same unsettling effect – indeed, the experts say that we are unable to smell more than three fragrances in quick succession before confusion sets in.

Smell within the creation

Within God's creation, smell has a particularly important part to play in how animals relate to each other and in how the food chain is connected. Many animals, of course, have a much more highly developed sense of smell than most humans, and can pick up scents on the wind that warn them of approaching danger or enable them to smell prey hiding away from them. Some animals have the ability to use smell intentionally, to ward off predators. It is not a good idea to frighten a skunk, for example. We have always known that dogs can smell much better than us. So we have exploited the capabilities of our dogs to use them to locate people and to sniff out dangerous and illegal substances. This extraordinarily enhanced smell world connects animals with changes in their environment over sometimes considerable distances: for example sharks can detect blood in the water at incredibly tiny concentrations. Smell is often the primary sense in the way many animals seek out and find mates. The release of pheromones into the air triggers mating behaviour that overrides all other considerations. Smell, perfume and fragrance also figure in our own sexual attraction and behaviour, as perfume companies are all too aware.

Oliver Sacks tells the story of a medical student who, having taken drugs, discovered that his sense of smell was extraordinarily enhanced. Because of this he became aware of a whole new way of experiencing the world and of relating to it through his senses.

'I went into a scent shop', he continued. 'I had never had much of a nose for smells before, but now I distinguished each one instantly – and I found each one unique, evocative, a whole world.' He found he could distinguish all his friends – and patients – by smell: 'I went into the clinic, I sniffed like a dog, and in that sniff recognised, before seeing them, the twenty patients who were there. Each had his own olfactory physiognomy, a smell-face, far more vivid and evocative, more redolent than any sight face.' He could smell their emotions – fear, contentment, sexuality – like a dog. He could recognise every street, every shop, by smell – he could find his way around New York, infallibly, by smell.[1]

The changing smells of life

Particular smells are intimately connected to who we are as human beings and there are particular smells which become deeply embedded in our memories about our creatureliness. For example, who can ever forget the distinctive smell of a newly-bathed baby? Is this the smell of incarnation? And what mother who has nursed her children will ever forget the pervasive smell of milk about her person, something that is perhaps troublesome at the time but is actually the smell of nurture. Children may find love and comfort in their own particular smell world and become distressed when their hygiene-conscious parents wash their favourite, much cuddled toy or blanket and make the calming, familiar smell of it disappear.

In heightened states of emotion, we give off and receive smells: 'the smell of fear' for instance. We react instinctively to the smell as much as the sight of blood, and during our lives we learn the smell of illness which emanates from the breath of a sick person and from the decomposing sweat of fevered skin. In looking after others, we instantly detect and react to alarming smells of illness, such as vomit and diarrhoea. Doctors often ask their patients if anything about their body smells different or unusual; forensic pathologists are aware that different smells can give clues as to how a person died.

For your love is better than wine, your anointing oils are fragrant, your name is perfume poured out.

Song of Solomon 1:2–3

The intimacy of love comes with its own set of special smells which are reinforced by closeness. This comes across in the scent imagery of the Song of Solomon.

If the one we love associates us with a particular perfume or fragrance, we are likely to wear it just for that person as a means of showing commitment and intimacy.

Read the Song of Solomon

Note all the references to scent and perfume.

❖ **How do these scent references remind us how wonderful human love is?**

❖ **How does this love poem of scents and fragrances remind us of God's love to us?**

❖ **Are there special scents and fragrances in your own relationships?**

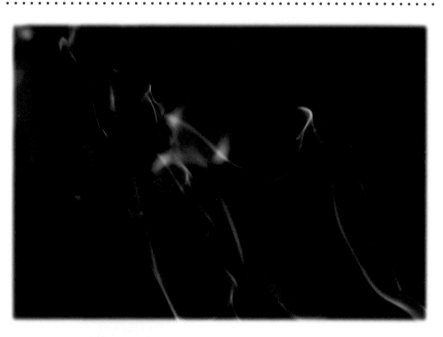

Death, too, has its own particular smell and in former times when death was not as hidden away and sanitised as it is in our contemporary society, a family could often tell when a death was imminent by smell alone. John Drane writes:

I remember becoming profoundly aware of this during a pastoral visit in Jamaica, when I was called to take the sacrament to an old man living alone in a remote spot in a wooden hut with no facilities, and in the final stages of a long illness. Though I had not known him previously, I could never forget the smell of death that lingered over him, even while still alive, and the consciousness that his personhood was diminished and would soon depart from his body.

Bereaved people sometimes cling onto a piece of their deceased relative's possessions for the very reason that they can – at least for a time – preserve a sense of their presence, through lingering smell.

He stretched out his hand and touched the smooth silk, the cloth, the muslin, the velvet, all those various textures. Stirred, the hanging folds gave out their perfume more strongly; he shut his eyes and inhaled her real presence. But what was left of her had been burnt, and the ashes were at the bottom of that pit in Lollingdon churchyard.[2]

Discover the smells of your home

Walk around your house and find all the products you have which carry a particular fragrance. Do you have a preference for a particular set of smells in your house? On your clothes? On your body? Are there smells you don't like? Are there different smell signatures for other members of your family?

Moving out: encountering God through smell

The Bible can help us begin to think about the place of smell in our personal spiritual journey as well as in our everyday life.

One of the things we don't often think about in studying and reflecting on scripture is how the different contexts must have smelled, even when the reference to smell is there. Often the smell of a situation contributes to the emotional content of the story, but we read intellectually and not with our senses fully engaged.

For example, in Genesis 27:27ff Jacob receives a blessing from his father Isaac in place of his brother Esau, because he is deliberately wearing his clothes:

> . . . he smelled the smell of his garments,
> and blessed him, and said,
> "Ah, the smell of my son is like the smell of
> a field that the Lord has blessed"

The emotional content of the scene is important. A significant rite takes place, but because Isaac is old and blind, the event is unfolded through a smell picture. There is savoury food, the smell of Esau's hunter's garments. There must have been the smell of emotions too: Jacob is terrified of discovery. Yet there is reassurance, joy and confidence in Isaac's mind as the familiar smell identifies the person with him as Esau, not Jacob. Yet so powerful is the smell picture that Isaac is tricked. With that reassurance comes the hoped for blessing.

One way of reading the Gospels might be to do so through the smells of different episodes. The nativity stories have an interesting mix: not only the smell of birth, but also of the shepherds and their sheep, and of the 'stable' (whether cave or stable, it would still have a distinctive fragrance). What must have the disciples smelled like, especially those who were fishing people? What would the centre of Jerusalem smell like? What would the prodigal have smelled like, living among pigs? What sort of smells accompanied the footwashing? What would Jesus himself have smelled like after riding the donkey or cooking the fish? What would his dead body have smelled like after it was embalmed with the spices?

Reflection point

Can you think of places in your faith journey so far where a smell was important or significant in some way?

Whence is that goodly fragrance blowing?

French carol

God's fragrance

What does God have to tell us about the importance of fragrance? We can see that smell has a particular role to play in the relationship between human beings and God. We can see this in many traditions. In ancient Greece, the Pythia at Delphi inhaled the fumes of burning laurel, Apollo's own tree, before going into her prophetic trance. In the Bible the smoke of burning spices and scented ingredients moves upwards and its motion and scent together create a sense of connection, as does prayer, between earth and heaven. The scent itself is supposed to concentrate our minds on what is holy and transcendent, to lift our thoughts beyond the mundane.

Smell offers a glimpse of something transcendent

If we think about our ability to smell in terms of our spiritual journey, we can see that the power of smell can make connections between the world we encounter as we breathe and the work of God within it. What kinds of smell help us to focus our hearts and minds on God and how can we use such smell to inform the way we try to share our faith with others?

There was certainly a consciousness in the Hebrew Scriptures that smell could have a transcendent dimension. The burning of incense was an ancient cultic practice, which the people of Israel probably took over from the Canaanites and we find it in the Bible as a feature of ritual:

> You shall make an altar on which to offer incense…Aaron shall offer fragrant incense on it; every morning when he dresses the lamps he shall offer it; a regular incense offering before the Lord throughout your generations. Exodus 30:1;7–8

Incense and oil

Similarly, we read the following instructions about holy anointing oil and making the special incense in the same chapter of Exodus:

The Lord spoke to Moses: Take the finest spices: of liquid myrrh five hundred shekels, and of sweet-smelling cinnamon half as much, that is two hundred and fifty, and two hundred and fifty of aromatic cane, and five hundred of cassia – measured by the sanctuary shekel – and a hin of olive oil; and you shall make of these a sacred anointing oil blended as by the perfumer; it shall be a holy anointing oil.

The Lord spoke to Moses: Take sweet spices, stacte [an oil of myrrh], *and onycha* [a spice from a mollusc found in the Red Sea], *and galbanum* [an aromatic resin from Asiatic plants], *sweet spices with pure frankincense (an equal part of each), and make an incense blended as by the perfumer, seasoned with salt, pure and holy…when you make incense according to this composition, you shall not make it for yourselves; it shall be regarded by you as holy to the Lord. Whoever makes any like it to use as perfume shall be cut off from the people.'* Exodus 30:22–5; 34–5; 37–8

What we learn from this is that there is a distinctive smell associated with holiness and with offering. When the people encounter the distinctive smell, they will know that they are in a holy place and among holy things. They will be encouraged to think about God. The instructions carry the sense of the preciousness of the oil and incense and the precise instruction that it is to be set apart from fragrances used in everyday life. It is not surprising then, that the precious gifts offered to the new-born Son of God are gold, frankincense and myrrh. When we re-enact the nativity stories in churches and schools, do we think to include the richness of the perfume that tells us we stand in the holy presence?

One of the challenges to us then is to think about how we recover the 'scent of holiness' with which to attract those searching for God. Certainly some Christians continue to use incense in their worship, but how far does the smell of incense tell people that something transcendent is happening/has happened here? When we use oil in the sacraments, does the idea, so present in Exodus, that the scent of it should lift ours hearts to heaven, *really* come across? Perhaps we should also take careful note that in the Hebrew Scriptures misusing the precious and holy incense and oil is a source of God's anger and disappointment as we see in Isaiah 1:13 and in Ezekiel 16:18 where the image is of using the perfume to prostitute oneself. If we are going to use fragrance in worship and use it to witness to others, then we have to treat it with the seriousness it deserves and not in frivolous or complacent ways.

Think about the smell of your church

Could the worship in your church be more 'fragrant'? Are there creative ways to use smell to set people's hearts on God?

Journey beyond smelling: smell and loss

We all know when we have a blocked nose with a cold and can't smell properly that the world seems flat and diminished. A particular problem with not being able to smell is that food becomes less appetising. Our ability to enjoy the world and interact with it is reduced or lost. The loss of the ability to smell therefore can shut down some avenues of spiritual perception and growth.

However, smell is important in other areas of loss and disability. For example, reminiscence therapy, using smell, is used to help people with Alzheimer's disease remember events and evoke memories. In helping people get through difficult times in their lives, or through particularly stressful situations, perhaps we too could do more to use smell to evoke hope, happy memory or peace.

There is a connection here with the renewed search for an 'embodied' theology and spirituality. Floyd Schaffer is a Lutheran priest in the USA, and a clown. He tells the story of how one day he celebrated the Eucharist as a clown, and included a 'flashpot' which evidently blew up with a puff of smoke at some point during the service. The intended liturgical purpose of this is not altogether clear, but one man in his congregation saw and smelled the smoke, and recognized it right away. To him, it was the smell of war, and in that instant he was taken back to the battlefield where so many of his friends had died. The connection on that occasion between this somewhat unusual smell of the Eucharist, and his life experience, became sacramental for him in new ways as he appreciated the relevance of the death of Christ in relation to his own prior experience.

Pause for prayer

Lord God,
You walk in all our memories
You know where we have been
What we have said, known and felt
Come to us in the scent we remember
The time when we walked with you
And know that we walk with you still
Amen

The double spiral: what do others smell?

Smell is intrinsic to who we think we are. The advertising industry pours millions into persuading us to buy cosmetics in order to ensure that at all times we will smell wonderful and alluring, encouraged by the evidence of our own self-consciousness, which tells us that we *do* smell different at the end of a long meeting in an unventilated environment from when we have just stepped out of the shower. In department stores there is often a number of staff offering you the chance to test different smells, and sometimes shoppers go that section just to spray a few lovely scents on themselves, not to buy anything. You can tell when you are approaching *Lush* from a considerable distance away. There are deodorants for every part of the body that might develop strong personal smells and anti-perspirants to stop smell formation in its tracks. The perfect body of the adverts not only looks good, it also always smells good. For many people their spiritual journey includes the pursuit of the lovely fragrance. Personal fragrances therefore sometimes have 'spiritual' names such as *Eternity*. This spirituality is reinforced by descriptions of the fragrances as being drawn from the sweet smells of nature, such as 'A fresh woody fragrance with notes of Bergamot, Lavender, Neroli and Amber'. And there is some evidence that by changing our smell we can indeed change how we feel about ourselves, and alter our moods. This is the basis of aromatherapy, with its use of essential oils to enable us to engage with our innermost beings, and to be empowered to be the best we can be. For many people, aromatherapy as given by a practitioner, or used at home, is an important way of getting rid of stress, relaxing, feeling good and opening the mind. Here is one description of the essential oils used in aromatherapy, which some therapists claim offers the possibility of being propelled into altered states of consciousness.

> **Essential oils have been used in healing since ancient times. They are found in different parts of the plant: petal (rose), leaves (eucalyptus), and roots of grass (vetiver), heartwood (sandalwood), and resin (frankincense). Often referred to as the 'life force' of plants, these oils have within them the unique complex properties of that plant in a concentrated form that can help the body holistically to heal itself. Through aromatherapy and using the essential oils we can improve both our emotional and physical health. The skin absorbs essential oils; therefore, massage is a very effective way of introducing them into the body. All essential oils are anti-bacterial, anti-viral or anti-fungal. Research has shown that aroma affects our emotional senses. This is because the olfactory nerves pass directly from the nose to the limbic system – the emotional centre of the brain. It is always important to enjoy the smell of the essential oil that we are using, as this will give us emotional balance.** [3]

Modern aromatherapy uses the same scents that occurs in scripture as a means of describing holiness and God's presence. The use of herb oils echoes the medicinal herb gardens of religious communities. What then do we have to do to re-establish the connections between the fragrances that are being used as a feel-good practice to gain 'emotional balance' and the pathway to God?

We are encouraged to extend this wonderful smell into our homes and belongings. Far from the odd joss stick, scented candles are particularly popular, as are perfume sticks and bottles which you can stand around the home or plug into an electric socket to scent your home. You must also seek out and destroy unpleasant smells, spraying your furniture and eradicating tobacco or animal smells. The toilet is a particularly sensitive area, with adverts saying worryingly 'what does your loo say about you?' and, more directly 'Pooh! That smells really bad!' You can add scented fabric conditioners to your clothes and put lavender-scented water in your iron. The way your house smells says something about your personality to your visitors. For many people, the scent of their environment is also a reflection of their spiritual search for peace and joy. Do we ever take proper account of this when we visit friends and neighbours and engage with them about it?

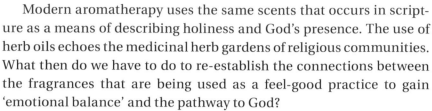

Exploring fragrance

Have a look round a chemist, supermarket or department store, or visit a shop selling aromatherapy oils. Try out some of the fragrances. Which ones, if any, connect to your own spiritual experiences and why?

Choose one fragrance in any form (such as a herb cushion) and use it as a background to meditation and prayer or bible study. See later whether the scent is enough to remind you of what you have been praying about or studying and to bring your mind to God.

Another way in which smell plays a part in people's spiritual journeys is where people seek out the smells of different locations. Restaurants and cafés may become spiritual homes for people because of their welcoming smells and people may be attracted to particular holiday destinations because their smells speak of 'paradise'. Different locations around the world certainly do have different smells. The fragrance of eucalypts in Australia or California is different from the smell of poverty, pollution, and smog that meets the visitor in cities like Metromanila in the Philippines or Mumbai in India. A western urban center like London

or New York smells different again, while the gentle fragrances of rural Jamaica or Hawaii after a shower of rain evoke their own distinctive atmosphere. The rich north smells different from the poor south, and the Arctic Circle different from the equator.

Smell and memory

Can you think of places you have visited, or holidays you have taken that have left you with a distinctive smell impression? What do you think 'paradise' smells like?

How might we make the connection for people when talking with them about favourite places, honeymoons or holidays?

She put her handkerchief to her nose. But the sharp rasping smell of the carcases leaked through the barrier of perfume, superimposing itself upon the sweetness, so that a respiration that began with *Quelques Fleurs* would hideously end with dead sheep or, opening in stale blood, modulated insensibly into the key of jasmine and ambergris.[4]

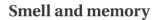

The evil stench

We associate bad or evil things with noisome smells, and stench. Hell was traditionally associated with the smell of brimstone – sulphur dioxide, the smell of rotten eggs. The presence of evil has often been associated with a foul odour, although Nietzsche also denounced the 'bad odour' of the Judeo-Christian tradition. The fragrance of holiness has always been contrasted with the smell of evil and perversion.

Smell, then, can call us to our duty as Christians to reconcile and transform the world. In former times, the privileged would carry a pomander – an orange stuck with cloves to ward off the noisome smell of a world without sewage disposal and treatment facilities. (For an unforgettable smell experience in a world full of stench transformed by a murdering perfumier, see Patrick Süskind's *Perfume*.) So, even today, how many people will stand on a tube train rather than sit next to the homeless person who smells bad because he has no other clothes to wear? Bad smells remind us of those whom God asks us to lift up from their oppression and set free. Being set free changes the smells they have access to and which they give out. So when we help those who are addicted to different substances, we set them free from the prevailing smell of the thing that has trapped them: the smell of alcohol, the smell of drugs, the smell of glue, the smell of prostitution. That work to set people free also requires that they become able to endure the smell of those addictions without finding them compelling. This may be true in our own lives if we are trying to cut down or give up addictions. A non-smoker will say that a heavy smoker smells like an ashtray, but the smoker will find the smell of a cigarette entirely wonderful. In giving up addictions, people may find the smell of tobacco or alcohol sets off their craving, so have to be helped to look for and enjoy other smells more than these. Where we encounter people dealing with the smell of

tobacco or alcohol, we can learn from them more about the smell challenges in our world. There is a smell of poverty, of famine, of sickness and of death in war and conflict. We are called as Christians to endure those smells and transform them into liberation, healing and peace and teach those around us what those abstract concepts really smell like, so that they become not just ideals, but a concrete reality. We can learn much from the stories of those involved in mission agencies of what it means to transform those smells and work to overcome them.

Prayer point

Lord God,

In the stink of rubbish tips where people make a living
In the stench of graves where people search for their dead
In the foul odour of disease where people are suffering
You are there
You are the fresh air.

Help us to make lives for the scavengers of rubbish
Help us to bring justice for the unknown dead
Help us to nurse and heal the diseased.

Help us to bring your fresh new life to the world
Amen

Jesus has taught us to transform that which is signified by evil stench into the fragrance of a new creation. For example:

Then Jesus, again greatly disturbed, came to the tomb. It was a cave, and a stone was lying against it. Jesus said, 'Take away the stone'. Martha, the sister of the dead man, said to him, 'Lord, already there is a stench because he has been dead four days.' Jesus said to her, 'Did I not tell you that if you believed, you would see the glory of God?' So they took away the stone…

The dead man came out, his hands and feet bound with strips of cloth, and his face wrapped in a cloth. Jesus said to them, 'Unbind him, and let him go.' John 11:38–44

Despite the smell of the rotting corpse, God's grace and healing power can transform what is broken and dead into what is truly alive. In Christian tradition, it is also often reported that holy women and men exude a sweet smell which overcomes the smell of death, so the fragrance becomes a sign of their victory over evil through their faith. For example, St Lawrence is said to have been martyred by roasting over a gridiron, but the smell of his burning flesh was replaced by a sweet smell instead. The bodies of other holy women and men are said to smell sweetly, as of roses, or violets, instead of smelling of putrefaction. Some appearances of the Virgin Mary as reported by those who have witnessed them, have included a sweet fragrance. This tradition is perhaps a sign of our task to rid the world of its 'bad smelling' evil and overcome it with the 'good smell' of transforming and reconciling lives.

As partners with God, we too must not be put off by the evil stench of corruption, but become witnesses to this same transforming power. This does not have to be some vast humanitarian project. Just helping an elderly or sick person clean their home, tidy their garden, wash their dog's dirty and matted fur, or do some washing and ironing for someone unable to do it for themselves can help to bring smell of God's love, care and concern into their lives.

Take a cautious walk

Have a walk round your local area. Where are the 'bad' smells in your own community? Where might you expect to encounter such bad smells? What could be done to change things?

The spirals entwined: the fragrance of others

Smell evokes memories

. . . he found the sun-warmed skin impregnated with a faint yet penetrating smell, at once salty and smoky, a smell that transported him instantaneously to a great chalk pit in the flank of the Chilterns, where, in Brian Foxe's company, he had spent an inexplicably pleasurable hour striking two flints together and sniffing, voluptuously, at the place where the spark had left its characteristic tang of marine combustion.

"L-like sm-moke under the s-sea," had been Brian's stammered comment when he was given the flints to smell.' [5]

We all have smells that connect us to particular memories. Perhaps the most famous example is the way the smell of the madeleine dipped in a cup of tea, recalled Marcel Proust to his childhood and every detail of a past life. The smell of freshly-mown grass, can evoke images of hard but rewarding work, or perhaps of lazy days spent in the park or countryside. The smell of the seaside, or of summer flowers might easily connect with idyllic childhood experiences. Or, more prosaically, the smell of polished furniture, or shoes, of washing and ironing, of new paint, of popcorn at the cinema, of the swimming pool – or of petrol or screenwash in the car, or the smell of the mechanic who services it … we all have our own stories.

Smell makes us aware of our surroundings, and produces many different emotions – fear, anticipation, expectation, happiness. All these things contribute to who we are and the stories which make up our personal narrative. They can also connect us with our fragility. Crime victims can sometimes identify their attackers by reference to their distinctive smell. We all intuitively recognize a smell that is 'not quite right' – electrical smells that warn of possible danger, or the smell

of a hospital. In fact, health and illness have many different fragrances associated with them. The burns unit of a hospital has a different smell from the maternity ward, while many healing medications also have a distinctive smell.

A poll to discover people's favourite smells had these results:

Sunday roast	25%
coffee	12%
barbecue	10%
mulled wine	2%
gingerbread	2%
popcorn	2%
cut grass	6%
honeysuckle	7%

In a newspaper article about these results, chef Richard Cawley said that the aroma of oven cooking took people back to more authentic times. 'I would have voted for the Christmas tree but it's great that so many people voted for the fabulous food smells.'[6]

What is interesting about this is the association with more 'authentic' times as the chef put it. The Sunday dinner was once as much part of the 'day of rest' as churchgoing. The mulled wine and the Christmas tree are part of the special smell of Christmas. We could perhaps pay more attention to the lovely smells associated with special times in the church calendar.

This poll also suggests that we, and all those others we encounter, inside and outside the Church, have common smell memories which we can share as part of our journey of mutual discovery of the world and all that is in it. This opportunity, beginning from a place of common experience, may allow us not only to speak of how smell leads us to God but we may also be surprised to learn where others have encountered God's presence through smell. What does the sheer pleasure of smelling something nice say about God? Eleanor Farjeon wrote 'praise for the sweetness of the wet garden' in her hymn *Morning is Broken*. What is the link from our smell memories to praising God? Perhaps the proper place for us to end up in our exploration of smell is in love and praise.

Reflection point

What smell memories, good or bad, do you have that would resonate with others? How could those memories be used to begin to listen to other's stories of the spiritual journey and to share our faith?

Using smell: journeying into Christian tradition

What does your church smell like?

What our churches smell like matters. For example, in the visitors book for 2004 in the small church of St John the Evangelist, Countisbury, Devon – to take just one example – there are a number of comments, such as 'impressive smell', 'smell of polish' and 'smell – warm and welcoming'. Conversely, the smell of dampness, musty paper, mould, ancient books or decaying flowers may create an impression of Church that is deeply off-putting to visitors and enquirers. The smell of a church that is loved and cared for can indicate to people that Christians are putting energy into their place of worship because this is a place where they meet the living God. So how can we work on what kinds of smell people encounter when they enter a church and what kinds of smell will help them encounter God's presence?

'Oh, I do admit,' cried Mrs Amberley, 'that a village congregation on a wet Sunday morning – well, frankly, it stinks! Deafeningly! But still…'

'It's the odour of sanctity,' put in Anthony Beavis…'I've suffered from it myself.'[8]

Stretch your legs

Go to your own place of worship and concentrate on what it smells like. What do you like or dislike about the smell? Is it comfortable, familiar and pleasing, or are there things you would like to change or put right? What would a stranger make of the smell of your church and what might they want to write in the visitors' book?

What do other places of worship in your area smell like? Do you know what the worship centres of people of other faiths smell like?

Since many people outside Christian tradition like to visit our churches, we could start with the smells of the environment outside the church building. The smell of new-mown grass in a churchyard speaks of love and care as well as evoking pleasant memories. Traditionally, religious communities often kept herb gardens for cooking and medicinal purposes and so the fragrant smells of lavender, sage and rosemary, associated with feeding and healing permeated the place of religious experience. Perhaps it would be possible to make a herb garden, or bring scented herbs, even in pots, into the church environment, so that people begin to make these connections with Church rather than something that is used in the home or to enhance private spiritual reflection. In a very restricted space, dried herbs in various forms could be enough to perfume the air. 🌐

Inside the church

If the church is the house of God, how do people know that this house is loved and cared for? The smell of polish or other cleaning products can speak powerfully to people of the activity of those who love this place and may prompt them to wonder why it is so loved. The smell of flowers is as evocative as it is in a home. Many faithful people give up their time to keep the church clean; perhaps more attention to be given to how their job provides a witness to Christian faith.

Similarly, it costs huge amounts of money for the upkeep of many historic church buildings, but perhaps there needs to be consideration of whether a 'bad' smell in a church in need of repair is preventing appreciation of other essential work that is being done. What priority should be given to making historic buildings smell more attractive to people?

Church facilities

More and more churches today have kitchens, toilets and 'living' areas for community groups. What do their smells say to people whose spiritual journeys bring them out of curiosity to the church door? What does it say to people if they can smell coffee or fresh bread in our place or worship, or if our toilets have a welcoming, fresh smell?

John Drane writes: At the start of my ministry I worked a lot with Chinese Christians. A typical Sunday service could last for anything up to three or four hours, and it would then be followed by a Chinese meal. One of the things we all looked forward to was the point when the smell of the food would invade the sanctuary, and signal that now was the time for community engagement. Though there was never this intention, I have often reflected on how closely that experience must have paralleled the experience of worshippers in the ancient temple at Jerusalem, where the smell of cooking food must have lingered everywhere in the atmosphere in much the same way as it does in some Asian temples today.

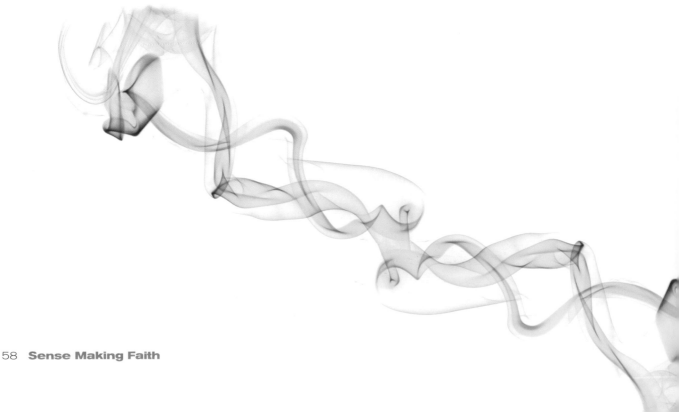

Summary of the journey into Smell

Where have we been?

This chapter has asked what it means to have the gift of smell and how that gift connects us intimately to the world around us, to each other, and to God.

❖ Smell is an important part of our existence as creatures, bringing us information about our environment, confirming ourselves as unique beings with our own individual smell and linking our selves with our history and our memories in a powerful way. As such, smell can therefore be an integral part of our spiritual journey and walk with God.

❖ Smell forms an important background to scripture, but it is one which we often ignore. People's experience is often richly steeped in the experience of smell in the biblical stories and informs the context and we need to become more aware of this, because it also connects with the smell experiences we, and people outside the Church, have in our own lives.

❖ Scripture also tells us that there is a link between smell, holiness and transcendence, such that the special fragrances of incense and oil can connect us to proper worship of God. How do we make people aware of that special connection in a society that is fascinated by perfume and fragrance, but is only dimly aware of its spiritual power in worship and sacrament?

❖ People outside the Church increasingly turn to fragrance for therapeutic reasons and to make statements about themselves and their environment. How can we understand what they are telling us by their scent choices and how can we make connections between the therapies and practices and the search for spiritual fulfilment?

❖ How does a greater awareness of the significance of smell in our own spiritual journey reveal to us the 'bad' smell of the world's inequality and injustice and how can we work to reconcile and transform it as a witness to others?

❖ How does the relation of smell to memory allow reflection on where God has been at work in our lives and how we may see God as having worked in the lives of others? What common smell memories allow us to share and learn from each other's stories?

❖ What do our churches smell like? And is that smell an invitation to explore and journey further, or is it off-putting to the spiritual seeker?

Reflect on 2 Corinthians 2:15–16

For we are the aroma of Christ to God among those who are being saved and among those who are perishing; to the one a fragrance from death to death, to the other a fragrance of life to life'.

The first task: to find
a frontier. I am not,
after all, everything.

Archbishop Rowan Williams

Journey into Touching

Starting the journey: what is touch?

A baby's first sensations are of touch. Even within the womb, babies reach out and explore their environment and their own bodies with their hands and feet. Through touch we establish physical contact of one body with another, or by one part of the body with another part of the same body. In most creatures the organ of touch is the skin, or the physical boundary of the body, with touch sensations relayed to nerve endings within the skin. We especially use our hands to touch things around us and have especially sensitive fingertips to explore our environment. Touch, however, plays a significant part in many living beings and some have specialised hairs such as whiskers. Many fish and other water creatures are exquisitely sensitive to vibrations in the water touching their bodies. Some plants also react to touch. Through touch we experience both pleasure and pain.

Touch tells us many things about the immediate nature of our environment, so there are many aspects to the sense of touch. For example, we react to temperature and will shiver in the cold and sweat in the heat (though with our eyes closed, we may not be able to distinguish freezing from burning sensations). We also respond to texture and shape, determining whether what we encounter is rough or smooth, soft or hard, sharp or blunt, curved or flat. Touch also tells us about pressure and weight (and perhaps the twist and tension) of what we encounter. We quickly build up ideas of what we like to touch and to feel. In children, the desire to touch may be very strong and feel entirely natural. How often do parents warn their children 'Don't touch!' in shops with breakable objects or when they want to stroke strange animals or play with candle flames? We perhaps forget how frustrating it is not to be allowed to touch, when others, especially children, realise how important touch is in answering their enquiries about the world.

We also keep in our heads a set of unpleasant sensations: things we would not 'touch with a bargepole'. Sometimes those unpleasant touch sensations get transferred to the idea of anything we don't like. People speak of spiders as 'hairy' when the average garden spider does not feel hairy at all. Similarly people think of snakes as slimy or slippery – 'slippery as a snake' – when snakes are typically smooth, cool and dry to the touch. The 'bushtucker' trials on the reality TV show *I'm a Celebrity Get Me Out of Here* involve ordeals of unpleasant touch experiences, things which make 'our skin crawl'. Further, we talk of people who live entirely in their heads as being 'out of touch', but we want to remain 'in touch' with people. Touch creates community; it consolidates relationships and reminds us that there are others out there. In total darkness, we will stretch out our hands and feel our way.

In touch between people, we also transmit our feelings and emotions. Two people holding hands will soon know whether one is feeling happy and loving, or cross and angry with the other person. Touch therefore forms part of deep communication and linkage between people. Friends or lovers who have fallen out very badly with each other will often avoid touching until the hurt is mended. Touching can be profoundly reconciliatory and revelatory. Moreover, in people with profound disability or learning difficulty, touch may

become the main 'language' by which they communicate their essential wholeness, personhood and humanity.

Touching is also the language of our intimacy, including sexual intimacy. Sexual relationships require honesty about the way we wish (or do not wish) to touch or to be touched. Different societies have always had dancing and courtship rituals to enable touching to take place safely and within agreed rules. Even within our own 'permissive' society magazines still pore over questions concerning what point in a new relationship you should kiss or have sex. Touch provides us with sexual languages: of desire, of love and of joy and gratitude. Touch teaches us about the physical body, our own and those of others; blind people often ask to touch people's faces to 'see' people, as well as to encounter other visual ideas such as colour. Different colours can sometimes feel 'sticky' or 'smooth' to blind people with that enhanced sense of touch which enables people to use Braille.

Touch also mediates to us the sacredness of our bodies and of our relation to God. Many people speak of the 'reverent' touch they feel is appropriate in holding a newborn baby or when a small child asks to hold their hand.

Reach out

Without moving, shut your eyes and see how many different types of surface are within reach. What do they feel like? What do your clothes feel like, the skin of your hands and face, your hair?

Moving out: touching God in our time

For Christians, touch is an important part of our spiritual life, since touch is involved at the major rites and ceremonies of the Church's life. This special touching takes place within a specific, safe, ritual space and is not just a matter of whether or not we touch each other during the Peace at church![1] At baptism, the sacrament comes to us at the most basic level in the feel of water on our skin, a touch experience which speaks directly to us of washing and becoming clean. If Christians come from a tradition where it is customary to make the sign of the cross with water at entering and leaving the church, this touch may bring back the memory of the baptismal promise. At confirmation, ordination, commissioning or consecration, hands may be laid on Christian people, in blessing and in welcome into the community. Touch is a sign of the apostolic succession. In marriage hands are touched and held.

On Ash Wednesday, Christians may be touched with ash in a way that reminds us that God has created us by 'getting his hands dirty'. Chrism oil is used in various acts of anointing and healing within the sacraments and the laying on of hands is an important part of Christian healing services. Rites of preparation for death involve touching the physical body in blessing and anointing. Touch mediates the sense of veneration: on Good Friday some Christians kiss the feet of Christ on the Cross; some priests kiss the altar, their stole, the gospel. On Maundy Thursday some also re-enact the washing of the feet by Jesus.

In the Eucharist, the priest or minister may demonstrate physical acts of touching which remind us of the experienced reality of the Last Supper. Hands are washed and dried, the elements are touched and handled. Hands perform the acts of consecration. In the Eucharist, too, Christians encounter the intimate act of feeding and this touch experience is translated into an understanding of Christ himself touching us and feeding us.

Our spiritual journeys, then, should be informed by touch, since it is deeply embedded in sacramental life. In Christian tradition touch has always been a part of the way we reach out to God in hope and prayer. For some Christians the touch of a rosary, or a holding cross is a way of keeping direct contact with the focus of prayer. Pilgrims especially may seek to touch things which remind them of the physical reality of Jesus and his disciples[4]. In former times, this may have resulted in devotion to relics and statues or to physically touching the stones of holy places. Pilgrims will still touch the foot of St Peter in Rome for example. But what else should we seek to touch in growing into a deeper knowledge and love of God and how does that experience of touch help us to share our faith with others outside the Christian tradition?

In Celtic spirituality, touching or holding natural objects such as stones can help to focus hearts and minds on God the creator of all. Incorporating the touch of the natural world within a spiritual life focused on Jesus can make sense to people outside the Church for whom the natural world is similarly important. Touch can establish connections where words or languages become confused.

What can one say about the the 'spiritual' significance of owning a piece of a pop star's clothing? It's not unusual for celebrities, such as Madonna, to auction their clothes for charity. Why do people want to own something they have touched or worn?

Following World War Two some German students volunteered to help rebuild a cathedral in England, one that had been badly damaged by the Luftwaffe bombings. As the work progressed, they weren't sure how to best restore a large statue of Jesus with his arms outstretched and bearing the familiar inscription, 'Come unto Me.' They were able to repair all the damage to the statue except for Christ's hands which had been completely destroyed. They wondered if these should be rebuilt. Finally, the workers reached a decision that still stands today. They decided to leave the hands off and changed the inscription to read: 'Christ has no hands but ours.'

Think about touch

In your home or your garden, so you have a favourite object you like to touch or hold?

What kinds of things give you pleasure to touch – playing musical instruments, handling cooking ingredients, weeding, brushing a child's hair?

❖ **What sorts of things would you *not* want to touch? Why not?**

What kinds of touch experiences have been important in your spiritual journey so far?

God's touch

Touch in creation

Scripture refers us to a number of ways in which God touches us. In the first instance, touch is imagined as a significant part of the act of creating. God gets 'his hands dirty' in the act of creation. Many people are familiar with Michaelangelo's image in the Sistine chapel of the creation of man in which Adam has just become a separate entity, his fingers stretched towards God's hand. In Genesis 2:7 'the Lord God formed man from the dust of the ground, and breathed into his nostrils

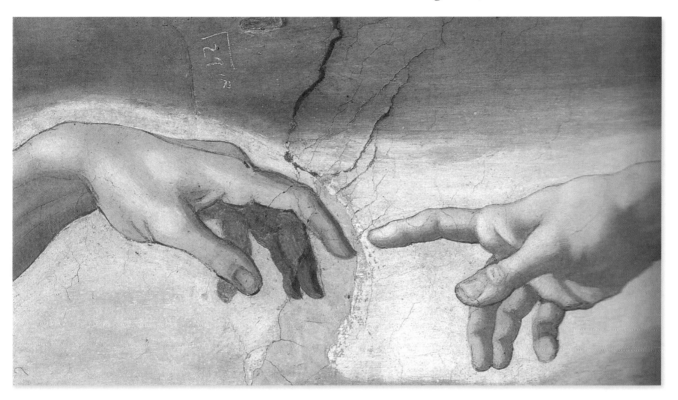

the breath of life, and the man became a living being'. In the creation of Eve, 'he took one of his (Adam's) ribs and closed up its place with flesh. And the rib that the Lord God had taken from the man he made into a woman' (Genesis 2:21–2). There are various ways of reading this account, but what is often overlooked is the powerful sense of intimacy as God gives Adam the kiss of life and reaches deep into his body for the material to create another, entirely separate living being. That sense of profound physical intimacy is passed over into the matter of right rela-tionship between the two beings. They indicate to all humanity that the deepest kind of intimacy involves becoming one flesh, when the flesh of the 'Other' is to be regarded with the same recognition and dignity as one's own. So it is then that Isaiah can proclaim 'Yet, O Lord, you are our Father; we are the clay, and you arc our potter; we are all the work of your hand' (Isaiah 64.8). We are imagined as shaped and moulded into our being, Jeremiah also speaks of being formed in the womb by God (Jeremiah 1.5). Yet God touches us but does not seek to constrain or hold. The touch of God is formation, and then liberation, though we are reminded that 'underneath are the everlasting arms'. The heavenly hope, as in the story of the Prodigal, is of the welcoming embrace.

Jesus encounters touch

In is unsurprising then, that when God becomes incarnate in Jesus Christ, touch should figure as such an important part of his life and ministry. We hear of Jesus touching people in the usual social ways, kissing people in greeting, embracing those whom he loved, serving them through touch, supremely in washing and drying their feet just as his own feet were anointed. We know that his early experiences are those of the physical reality of touch: like any Jewish baby of his time, he is wrapped in swaddling bands (Luke 2:12); he is circumcised (Luke 2:21). He is taken into Simeon's arms and held even as God is praised (Luke 2:28). Similarly, at Jesus' baptism, touch experiences are significant. He feels the water on his body and encounters the Spirit 'descending like a dove and alighting on him' (Matthew 3:16). At his crucifixion, Jesus' body also endures appalling and abusive touch as he is flogged, crowned with thorns and finally crucified. No one who has seen Mel Gibson's 2004 film *The Passion of the Christ* is left in any doubt as to what those final hours of being touched by violence was like.

Jesus touches others

In Jesus' ministry then, touch becomes an important sign of the real physical connection between human beings and God. People brought 'little children to him in order that he might touch them' (Mark 10:13). When the disciples tried to prevent the children coming near, Jesus 'took them up in his arms, laid his hands on them, and blessed them' (Mark 10:16). There is nothing casual or incidental about this touching; it is a sign that God is not some distant untouchable being, but intimately involved with the physical world. So we too must become as little children, trusting God and reaching out in relationship.

Supremely, Jesus heals by means of touch, laying his hands on people in pain or suffering, taking people by the hand and raising them up to take their place in the world again (eg Mark 9:27). We hear in the gospels how people also struggle to touch Jesus themselves, believing that connection will have powerful spiritual effects, will bring blessing upon them and heal their pain. The resurrection appearances, in which Jesus is clearly not a filmy ghost or a vague spirit, requires us to face up to the physical reality of the resurrection body and the idea that heaven is *more* real than our existence now. However hard it is for us to grasp this theologically or imaginatively, it is irrefutably present in the experience of the Eucharist. We experience the touch of real things to be taken into our physical bodies under the words of Christ about his own physical body: 'This is my Body' and 'This is my Blood'.

This forms the background for our own understanding of touch in our lives and how through touching others in loving and healing ways, we may find Christ in them and they may encounter him in us.

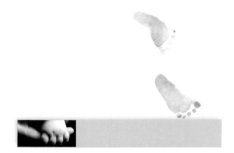

Pause for prayer

Lord,
You knew the touch of love.
You knew the touch of friendship
You endured the kiss of betrayal
You endured the crown of thorns

Help us to touch others with your love
Help us to touch others with your friendship
Help us to heal the wounded hearts
Help us to heal the scars and hurts

For your name's sake
Amen

Journey beyond touching: being untouchable

Scripture tells us that in the ancient biblical world ritual religious behaviour discriminated between what is 'clean' and 'unclean'. Indeed the book of Leviticus lays out clearly what kinds of contact are permitted and what is not, and what you should do about it if you come into contact with what is 'unclean'. There were very good reasons for these rules, which, in a society with little medicine, were designed to protect people from illnesses known to be contracted from food such as undercooked pork and shellfish, and to control the spread of disease. The rules about what was 'unclean' therefore instigated a form of hygiene control and quarantining of contagion. If people became unclean for various reasons, such as touching a dead body, they would have to 'purify' themselves in order to rejoin the community. This reminds us that touch is not universally good. If we touch without accepting responsibility we can also contract and transmit disease. In a western culture where STDs are rife and the world is afflicted with HIV, it requires us to think carefully about how we think about the moral responsibilities of touching and intimacy. Touching should be for healing, not harm, so when is it right to 'refrain from embracing'?

However the concepts of 'cleanness' and 'uncleanness' also meant that certain people became permanently unclean, because they could not purify themselves. Such people could not be touched as their uncleanness would be passed on, so they became outcasts, permanently excluded from the community. People with leprosy and other diseases were especially vulnerable. This meant that power could be abused within the community, to set up an unjust stratification of society in which some elements were pure, clean and holy (and therefore 'owning' God), and other elements were unclean, untouchable and beyond God's pale.

Jesus revolutionised this unjust system by breaking through the taboos about 'uncleanness'. When his disciples broke the hygiene rules, he countered with an argument about the purity of the human heart before God and caused scandal by touching, being touched by, and healing the untouchable, the permanently impure: lepers, people

with mental illness, the woman with the flow of blood. When Jesus healed them, their 'uncleanness' fell away from them and they could be restored to the community. Thus his healing touch was more than an act of compassion and love; it was also a challenge to the community that such people be readmitted to the realm of the touchable.

The story of the Prodigal Son is the more moving because of the restoration of the son who has become untouchable in his degradation among the pigs. Yet his father 'ran and put his arm around him and kissed him' (Luke 15:20) restored him and set a feast for him. This story presents a continuing challenge to us today, especially as Jesus suggests to his followers that whenever we break one of our own taboos about reaching out to those we would rather not touch, the person we encounter is Jesus himself (Matthew 25:34–40). So Peter's dream in Acts 10 comes with the words 'what God has made clean, you must not call profane' (v15).

What if God were one of us
Just a slob like one of us
Just a stranger on the bus
Trying to find a way home

Joan Osborne, *One of Us* from the *Relish* album 1995

Touch and taboo

What kind of touch taboos do you have?

Who are the 'unclean' people in your community? What would it take to restore them to fullness of life among us, as Jesus did?

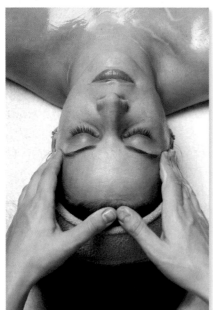

Abusive touch

Touch is one of the most important senses for determining right relationship. Touch is a powerful indicator that we are loved. We feel safe, secure and happy when those we love hold us, embrace us, kiss us, stroke us, soothe us, comfort us. But that loving, healing touch can only come to us with the permissions we grant for particular people to cross our physical boundaries and invade our personal space. Some of those permissions are now closely bounded in our society. We may permit doctors to touch us intimately, but women patients will need a chaperone to prevent any opportunity for abuse or claims of abuse. It is more difficult these days for teachers to find appropriate ways to console children by means of touch. We now live in a culture which has more and more problems about the acceptable parameters of touching. Touch permissions are different for every person and may be closely related to the spiritual journey. There can be people in our churches and communities who suffer silently from a legacy of forced, commanded touching which interferes with their worship and has perhaps contributed to the popularity of quiet, formal early morning services, especially in cath-

The policeman took hold
of my arm and lifted
me onto my feet.
I didn't like him
touching me like this.
And this is when I hit him.[2]

edrals where it is possible to be more anonymous. For many, perhaps most, Christians, sharing the peace is a friendly and affirming experience. For others, it is a moment in the service they dread. Some people are easily 'touchy-feely' and give and receive touch gladly. Other people hate to be touched and shrink from the contact readily offered by others. How, and how often, we wish to be touched can also change according to how we are feeling. We might feel less inhibited about touching other people after a few drinks at a party; we might want people to leave us well alone when we are ill or frozen with misery or bereavement. The book of Ecclesiastes (3.5) reminds us that there is 'a time to embrace and a time to refrain from embracing'. Jesus, after his resurrection, asked Mary not to touch (or hold on to) him, *noli me tangere* (John 20.17).

The other side of this particular coin is the way that touch can certainly be abused. In engaging with this particular physical sense we cannot ignore the way people may abuse their power to touch people in inappropriate and abusive ways. We most readily think of this in terms of sexual abuse, and certainly we cannot avoid confronting the way people have been traumatised and their lives ruined by unwelcome invasion of the most ruthless kind. But there are other kinds of abusive touch, all involving the use of power by one person or persons to overcome others. Abusive touch includes physical as well as sexual violence, cruelty (including gratuitous cruelty towards animals), torture, bullying and physical humiliation, invasive touch of all kinds. Consequently, Christians have to be very careful about the kinds of touching we offer to people out of their love for them and what those people might understand by it. We also see in our society, the problem reversed. Touching is a sometimes a dangerous negotiation within people, and signals become horribly mixed. Sometimes friendly and caring touching ends up being put in the same box as genuine abusive harassment. Or, we can simply not realise what we are doing to people.

Mark Haddon's novel *The Curious Incident of the Dog in the Night-Time* tells the story of a young person with Asperger's syndrome who is greatly disturbed by the deliberate killing of a dog. People with Asperger's or autism may find any of the physical senses conveys far too much information for them to cope with, and in the case of touch, it can be deeply distressing, unpleasant and frightening. For such people, ordinary loving touch can constitute abusive touch. So too, people or animals who have been hurt, traumatised, frightened or who are suffering in other ways, may not be able to endure too much touching. We have a responsibility in using our natural empathy to find out what other people can bear. Mark Haddon's story gives an example of the way in which we must find ways to connect appropriately with those who have been hurt or who cannot bear our touch:

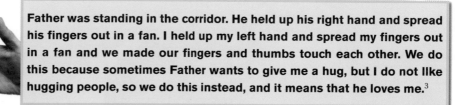

Father was standing in the corridor. He held up his right hand and spread his fingers out in a fan. I held up my left hand and spread my fingers out in a fan and we made our fingers and thumbs touch each other. We do this because sometimes Father wants to give me a hug, but I do not like hugging people, so we do this instead, and it means that he loves me.[3]

Oliver Sacks tells the moving story in *An Anthropologist on Mars* of a woman with Asperger's syndrome who built herself a machine within which she could control the sense of being squeezed and hugged.[4] Although she longed to be embraced, she could not bear to be so touched by human beings. How might we respond to those who long for contact but cannot bear our touch?

A few weeks ago, I took part in a discussion that involved a number of people working with children and young people who suffer from different forms of 'autism' – the kind of disorder that seems to cut people off from ordinary communication and shows itself in strange repetitive behaviours and sometimes in violent outbursts. We watched a video showing the work of one of the most experienced therapists in Britain, and then heard her talking about what she is trying to do with her methods.

The first thing we saw on the video was a young man, severely disturbed, beating his head against a wall, and then walking fast up and down the room, twisting and flicking a piece of string. The therapist's first response was strange: she began to twist and flick a piece of string as well. When the young man made a noise, so did she; when he began to do something different, like banging his hand on a table, she did the same.

The video showed what happened over two days. By the end of the two days, the boy had begun to smile at her and to respond when touched. A relation had been created....

. . . we should think of God watching us moment by moment, mirroring back to us our human actions – our fears and our joys and our struggles – until he can at last reach out in the great gestures of the healing ministry and the cross. And at last we let ourselves be touched and changed.

Archbishop Rowan Williams, Christmas Message to the Anglican Communion 2004.[5]

In this story, Rowan Williams gives us a model of connection and healing which is the exact opposite of abusive and frightening touch. In the end, as we struggle with our broken world, God touches us. Our task then, is to allow God to touch us, mirror us and create relationship and, in our turn, to engage with others and be their mirror. But are we ready for the responsibility that such healing touch lays upon us?

That professional touch

Make a list of all the 'professional' people who touch you: hairdressers, doctors, dentists, chiropodists, manicurists, etc.

What kinds of touch are pleasurable in these situations?

Which kinds of touch are not pleasurable but necessary?

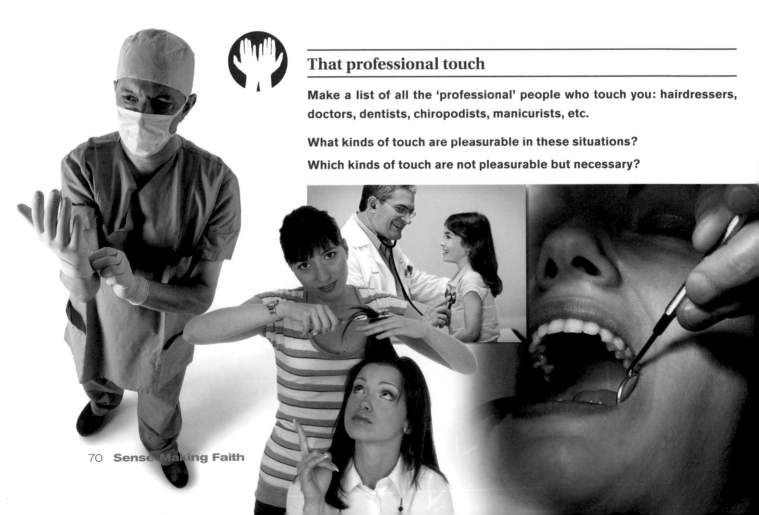

The double spiral: what do others touch?

Touch is increasingly important in the spiritual journeys of people both inside and outside the Church. We can look at two particular aspects of this touch: the touching of the physical body by other people, and the things we choose to touch us in our everyday lives.

Being touched

There are very many practices and therapies which involve touch. Some of these practices are designed to help people with ailments, but very many are designed to help people feel relaxed, peaceful and content. Some people's idea of luxury or being 'pampered' will include a sauna, enjoying the sensation of sweltering heat on the skin and followed by a refreshing coldness, but more particularly, people enjoy one of the many forms of massage currently available and which require practitioners to have an underlying knowledge of the body's response to different forms of touch. For example, here is a description of Indian Head Massage.

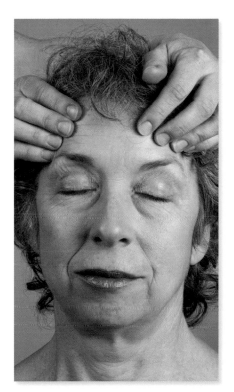

Although it is fairly easy to learn the basics of Indian Head Massage, this form of massage should not be taken lightly, it is both subtle and deep leaving the client feeling deeply relaxed, rejuvenated and deeply affected.

An Indian Head Massage generally starts with the client sitting in a comfortable chair for the duration of the massage.

There is no need to remove clothing although it should be noted that a cotton top or T shirt is probably the most comfortable thing to be wearing. Some clients prefer to remove their top to prevent any oil staining.

Treatment normally begins with a deep kneading and probing of the neck and shoulder muscles. At times similar to Osteopathy but with no crunching or cracking of joints. The head is then worked with the scalp being squeezed, rubbed, gently tapped and prodded. The hair is briskly tussled and gently combed.

Pressure points are gently worked on and the ears are tugged and pressed. Lastly the practitioner moves to the face, working with acupressure points to help relieve any sinus pressure, stimulate the circulation and increase alertness. The face is also very gently stroked.

Once a massage has been complete the client should remain at rest for at least 20 minutes.[6]

The sheer number of touch verbs in this description should reveal why such massage is very popular with people. The aim is to reach a state of deep relaxation and freedom from anxiety. It is unsurprising then, that many people use massage of some part of their body as part of their spiritual journey, the practice taking them to a place of self-knowledge and experience that enables them more easily to explore their life with God. This also means that non-Christian practitioners of touch therapies such as reflexology may come to learn more of people's spiritual journey that we do within the Church.

Two stories from a beauty therapist

A beauty therapist had an elderly lady for a client who needed to help to look after her feet and cut her toenails. The elderly lady enjoyed

the ministrations of the beauty therapist particularly because her feet were washed, dried, massaged, rubbed with peppermint oil and had her toenails cut and painted. 'You make my feet look beautiful again'. One day, this process led the elderly lady to comment on how her late husband had used to rub her feet when she was unwell and whether she would ever be with him again in an afterlife. The beauty therapist's touch recalled her husband to her and led her to speak of her hope of heaven and to rediscover the touch of love and reconciliation.

On another occasion, the same beauty therapist had a young female client who wanted a bikini wax so she could look good on holiday. However during the process the client started to cry. The therapist was worried that she had hurt her, but the client explained that the therapist's touch had set off a memory about being used and dumped by a boyfriend and led to a conversation about why the young woman wanted to look good – for herself or for others, and what a loving relationship would really mean.

Remoulding the clay, 'improving' our bodies

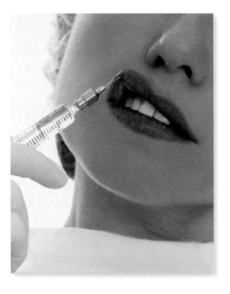

If people's spiritual journeys now also include the need for touch experiences to relax and think more deeply, they are also complemented by pressure to do other things to their bodies to improve on what is 'God given'. What is interesting is that in today's society some of these involve discomfort or downright pain, at least in the first instance, but this is seen as a necessary evil in order to say something about the person you are. In one strand of Christian tradition, wearing an uncomfortable itchy shirt was seen as a way of subduing the flesh and preventing Christians from becoming complacent (one such famous person to wear such a shirt was St Thomas à Becket). This was seen as a way to holiness. Today, undergoing painful procedures and wearing uncomfortable clothes and shoes tends to be just a by-product of what fashion gurus tell us looks glamorous or sexy. We will endure painful touch, by shaving or waxing, or endure blisters from high heeled shoes, we can have injections of a toxin to stave off wrinkles, while more and more men and women now put cosmetic surgery on their Christmas list as a means to the end of looking lovelier for longer. What does this tell us about the spiritual journey and where in the community of the beautiful do people fit who cannot live up to these exacting standards? After all, why is Bridget Jones funny? 🌐

Think about touch

A group of young teenagers were discussing the glamour model Jordan (Katie Price) and the surgery to increase the size of her breasts. One of the teenagers commented on the fact that Jordan's son Harvey was born with sight problems. 'When are they going to fix *him*?'

Another in the group pointed out that Jordan's whole career has been about being seen, but her own son was cannot see. 'He can *touch* her!'

❖ **What is the difference between enhancement and healing?**
❖ **Who wants to touch the 'real' Katie Price?**

. . . .

But perhaps even more fascinating in the matter of touch and discomfort is the interest in tattoos and body piercing, which require asking a practitioner to run inks under the skin to make pictures, words or patterns, or to make holes in just about any part of the body including tongues and genitalia. Getting your ears pierced was once a female teenage ritual, now it is not uncommon to see parents bringing their babies for ear piercing, while the range of piercing and body jewellery available to both men and women is as creative as it is wide. Of course, tattooing and piercing are common in many cultures, but in our western society it has become linked with particular statements of identity: who I am (including 'this is my sexuality') and where I am going. David Beckham, for example, adds new tattoos to his body to celebrate significant life events such as the birth of his sons. It can therefore become possible to 'read' a person's life from their body, but instead of writing in a diary or taking photographs, that person records important events or feelings via a touch experience. How big a deal this is for some people can be judged from *You who have ears to hear* in *Good News* issue 43 Autumn 2000, p. 8.

Touching Jesus

Jesus was also pierced – by nails and a sword – and his resurrection body bears the marks of his piercing. There was an invitation to look upon him and the invitation to *touch*.

He said to Thomas, 'Put your finger here and see my hands. Reach out your hand and put it in my side. Do not doubt, but believe.' Thomas answered him, 'My Lord and my God!'
John 20:27–8

The text doesn't actually say that Thomas touched Jesus although he was invited to do so. The picture clearly understands that he did.

What do you think happened?

What not to wear

We are naked apes. Our bare skin brings us many touch sensations, so in today's society, there is great preoccupation with the things we put on or next to our skin. Every morning, we have to make touch choices as we get up and choose clothes for the day. The clothes encase us, touch us intimately. We quickly become aware of the kinds of fabrics we like to wear 'for work' or for 'going out' or for 'staying in'.

Clothes become part of spirituality because we inhabit them, we 'indwell' our clothes. Clothing and fashion are very important to many people, prompting them to answer the question 'what do your clothes say about you?' For example, Goth culture invests a great deal of importance in clothing which is linked with a particular kind of spiritual outlook.

Christians talk about 'inhabiting' and 'indwelling' as theological words, but many people understand these concepts naturally and instinctively as they choose what to wear (and what not to wear). Some people like to wear clothing that is artificially ripped or torn so that the body that indwells the clothing shows through. The clothing is revealed as a layer that contains 'the real me'. How does this relate to boy in the shirt who ran away naked, or to the stripping of Jesus and the dicing for his clothes? Human beings crucified a naked God, whose inner self was ultimately revealed. A penitent thief and a centurion saw that inner self and recognised Jesus for themselves. What connections can we make here?

Important occasions in the spiritual journey are often accompanied by special clothing. The choice of bridal dress for example, has become a ritual in itself, invested with sacred importance, as a quick flick through any bridal magazine will soon demonstrate, but do we as Christians spend any time investigating the spiritual significance of something as apparently materialistic as the bridal gown when people come to church to be married? In some traditions, the baptised are clothed with a white garment and we readily acknowledge the spiritual symbolism involved in that action. Why don't we transfer that understanding to other kinds of dressing up? There can be spiritual significance embedded in that choice of a white dress, the other wedding colours chosen, the touch experiences of the hair and make up ritual, which we never hear about because we don't ask.

We should be interested in the way people reinvent themselves by the way they engage with fashion and fabric, the coverings that touch their bodies. We should also look carefully at questions of identity, how people use touch experiences to proclaim who they say they are under God.

Think about clothes

Why do people sometimes find it hard to throw away clothes?

What's special about your favourite clothes?

Could you tell someone a story about what you wore on your wedding day (or at someone else's wedding or on another special day) which focuses what you felt about the occasion itself?

The spirals entwined: touching others

The idea of people experiencing touch in Church has a difficult history. In some traditions, receiving the host on the tongue rather than touching it was mandatory. In some congregations exchanging the peace with a handshake is still groundbreakingly new. In some churches, furious handwiping goes on before the task of filing out and having to shake hands with the minister….But touch is fundamental to our sense of community, of meeting and greeting people. Touch creates community. At the end of a football game, players exchange shirts with the opposing team as an act of goodwill. Friends and siblings borrow each other's

clothes. Clubbers take off their shirts to experience the community of dancers. Yet very often we are most adept at stylised greetings and air kissing…

Miriam Kings' installation in St Mary's, Islington: the face of Christ composed of pieces of clothing.

Engagement with the spiritual journeys of people outside the Church requires us to take seriously the issue of how we touch others and what kinds of touch we experience. At a time when churches debate whether to do away with religious clothing, it throws into focus the traditional importance of ritualistic clothing with its evocations of mystery and symbolism. In thinking about clothing and fabrics we need to see how we can make more use of our Christian tradition and honour it. This includes engagement with, but not selling out to pop culture because it's cool or trendy to do so. In mission, although we are constantly exercised by issues of accessibility, we should stay in the tradition so that it can be recognised and encountered by others. This can communicate to people clear signals about who we are and what our own spiritual journey is like.

However Christians need permission to play with the tradition without being censured for ruining it. We have a culture of different 'uniforms' in our churches, and people could be encouraged to get beyond this. Our own clergy receive a particular 'culture' back from those who train them.

Tactile experience

What fabrics do you have in your church?

How many of them have you touched/can you touch?

If you decorate the Church at Christmas/Easter/Harvest Festival, do the displays include things that can be touched, encountered, played with?

Using touch: journeying into Christian tradition

The things which touch our skin are important in our society, but Christians don't necessarily think of them as connected with our spirituality. After all Jesus himself tells us that we shouldn't be bothered by what we wear (Matthew 6:28–30). One result, which was surely not intended by Jesus, is that we don't pay much attention to touch experiences. It is clear that in many churches, where there are fabrics, we are not supposed to touch them. In some churches there are beautiful and intricate altar frontals and falls, or banners and ornamental sewing, but they are to be looked at rather than encountered. Vestments are put on over other clothing. We tend to sit on hard pews or chairs, rather than on cushions or other fabrics. The sensation of immediate touch is for the most part excluded from our worshipping life.

This is odd because a tradition of making fabrics has long been part of church life. Many churches have sewing or knitting circles or other fellowship groups in which kneelers or banners are made. This tradition of making and creating new things presents us with an exceptional opportunity, but this opportunity comes from including touch. The following account of a spiritual journey through touch encounter with fabric illustrates this:

The Garments of Gethsemane 🌐

The Revd Peter Privett's journey began during a clergy/lay conference in Hereford diocese. He was asked to focus on the meaning of suffering and the experience of Gethsemane. The conference was principally cerebral, without visual or other means of participation. Peter worked with the liturgy people, aware that the events of September 11th 2001 were on people's minds. He decided he would make the focus on suffering, using textiles with contemporary images. The initial garment didn't work and he got frustrated and angry with it, finally tearing it. He realised that garments could have holes in them and people could be encouraged to meditate reflectively on the garments. However he realised that the inclusion of contemporary images could dictate what people should feel about them. His *Godly Play* experience suggested that encouraging people to ask open-ended questions was a more fruitful way. (*Godly Play* is a process for sacramental worship designed for children by Jerome Berryman which encourages wondering, dreaming and creative engagement with story, prayer and Eucharist.)

The very process of making the garments was open ended, in that Peter started off by not knowing what to do or where to go with the project, and so began by exploring. The red garment brought to mind the book of Amos, the purple one the Psalms with their linen and sackcloth. His emotional response brought to mind Jeremiah. As he worked he discovered that he could work more and more with the emotional response evoked by scripture. The green garment, made of recycled fabrics and evoking the natural world, brought to mind Isaiah and the beginnings of restoration. The white garment, a white coat, made of strips of embroidered linen with a scarf of nails piercing the fabric, came to symbolise the Resurrection and was indeed finished

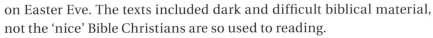

on Easter Eve. The texts included dark and difficult biblical material, not the 'nice' Bible Christians are so used to reading.

Therefore making the garments became in itself part of the Lent and Holy Week process, a different way of experiencing the events leading up to Easter. The fabrics allowed other ways into the experience: you can touch them, feel them, hold them, wear them. We are enjoined to 'put on Christ' like a garment and Peter's garments enable people to get to the heart of this.

During the conference, one garment was carried to the chapel each day as a focus for the Eucharist. The white coat enfolds all the other colours, the red, purple and green. As installations, the garments stand about eight feet tall on easels. People are now able to take them away to use. They are displayed in Leominster Priory when not in use. People are constantly thinking of new ways of using them. The garments enable ministry: they hold pain, give voice to the screams of others; they provide a means of discernment and an enfolding of those suffering.

The texts on the garments come in different forms. Some are written, some embroidered, some painted. Some look like graffiti. The texts are open-ended, but four boxes were provided with the texts inside. Peter also provided a booklet for people's comments: some were angry and negative, others deeply appreciative. Some people were amazed to learn that the words actually came from the Bible. So the garments provided a focus to talk and discuss scriptural texts and particular verses.

Peter said that his experience of *Godly Play* had given him a sense of the mystery and importance of story. It brings the recovery of something which speaks deeply. We should not explain the stories until all the mystery has gone away, but keep the sense of the enigmatic and mysterious so that people feel there is more to discover. With the garments, their colours speak first. It is also interesting that Peter had found people swearing at the garments – human experience speaks back. Just as mission starts with the human condition, so Peter's anger and frustration paved the way for the creativity.

The garments have also proved helpful in engaging those with special learning needs, where direct tactile contact allows engagement to take place.

Use the Bible

Find a favourite Bible story.

What touch experiences might have been involved in that story?

Find some fabrics or other materials which might convey those experiences.

How would you retell the story in terms of what was touched?

Or: **Find four fabric pieces or ribbons or other textiles in the liturgical colours, red, green, purple, white/gold.**

Handle the textiles and think about the colours in relation to the story of Jesus.

What fabric goes with what part of that story in your mind (you don't have to go with the 'official' version)?

What biblical texts or prayers come to mind?

Summary of the journey into Touching

This chapter has asked us to reflect on what it means to touch and to be touched.

❖ What does it mean to experience touch? Touch is especially important in telling us about our environment. Our skin is our physical boundary and the place where our exploration of the world starts. Touch is the basis of relationship, the way we encounter what is 'other'

❖ Touch is an integral part of the sacramental life of the church. Baptism, confirm-ation, marriage, extreme unction, ordination – all these involve sacred acts of touching. How much attention do we pay to the significance of touch at these times?

❖ The creation around us, as well as our own bodies speaks to us of God's touch. In the incarnation Jesus came to us as one experiencing touch and whose own capacity for touching others is shown to us as acts of healing and blessing. In the Eucharist we also have the opportunity to engage in all the different ways God touches us.

❖ Throughout history some people have become 'untouchable'. Such people are cut off from society and community and only touch can restore them. Jesus is the model for this recuperative and restorative touch. But are we really willing to copy his example and touch society's untouchables ourselves?

❖ Touch can also be abused. Touch carries with it great responsibility. Some people have been hurt and damaged by the touching of others. Other people cannot bear to be touched. Where is appropriate healing touch in these situations and how does that relate to the way God seeks to reach out, touch and heal us?

❖ How do we make sense of the way people treat their bodies? What does the interest in different kinds of practices and therapies which involve touch mean to people? How do we make sense of the way people feel they can 'remake' their bodies and the way in which they adorn them with tattoos and jewellery? What is the spiritual significance of clothes and fashions?

❖ Why is touch sometimes difficult for Christians in worship? What do we need to learn, or what permissions do we need to use this physical sense to create our own community and sense of sharing?

❖ What creative possibilities are there for the use of fabrics and touch experiences within Church? We can learn to indwell our touch experiences in such as way as to mirror the indwelling of the Spirit. Peter's story gives us one such example.

Reflect on this passage of Scripture

A man of the city who had demons met him.
For a long time he had worn no clothes…
Then people came out to see what had happened
And when they came to Jesus
They found the man from whom the demons had gone
Sitting at the feet of Jesus
Clothed and in his right mind.
Luke 8:27; 3

Journey into Tasting

The strip of red flesh
lies still, absorbs, silent; speaks
to all the body.

Archbishop Rowan Williams

Starting the journey: what is taste?

Our tongues are the organs of taste, containing taste buds which detect and respond to dissolved molecules and ions (as opposed to smell which works with taste by responding to airborne molecules). The taste buds respond to a limited range of actual 'tastes' of which the traditional ones are: salty, sour, bitter, and sweet. According to some scientists we also have a fifth taste: 'umami' – a response to the salts of glutamic acid, such as monosodium glutamate (MSG), aspartates etc.

Explore your taste

Taste a *very small* amount of the following substances, drinking water in between:

A few grains of salt

A few grains of sugar

A granule of instant coffee

A drop of pure lemon juice

What are your feelings and reactions to these 'pure' tastes?

Do the tastes make you think of anything or any particular experiences or memories?

Which of the taste experiences would you want to repeat and which not?

. . . .

We respond to these primary tastes because we need to know what we are putting inside our bodies, so taste is directly related to what we eat. We respond to the sweet taste of sugars because we need carbohydrates, and to salt because the body also requires salt. The umami response is said to detect important amino acids. The bitter and sour responses are to tell us what *not* to eat – because most poisons taste bitter and rotting food generates acidic products which taste sour. In the first instance then, tasting is a regulator of what is good or bad for us. It reminds us to pay attention to feeding ourselves appropriately and not to make ourselves ill.

The *experience* of taste is another matter. The experience of taste is related to what food looks like, its texture, temperature and its smell as well as the 'actual' taste of the food. It is very difficult to taste food properly if your other senses aren't working correctly. You may well lose your appetite if you have a cold, but eventually you will start to enjoy food again. It is quite a different matter if you lose your colour vision, eating grey looking food is very difficult indeed.

Activity Point

You will need a number of small glasses and a rotating board like a carousel. Put a few drops of coffee and a few drops of tea, *or* red and white wine, *or* brandy and whisky into the glasses. Put the glasses on the carousel, close your eyes and rotate the carousel so you don't know which glass is which.

Hold your nose very firmly closed, keep your eyes closed, and sip from the different glasses. Can you tell which is which?

Do the same experiment with some grated apple and grated onion.

There is also a sense in which taste is more than straightforward feeding or experiencing savours. Babies 'taste' the whole world, putting everything they encounter in their mouths and learn about their environment by sucking, licking and chewing it. Animals lick their newborn or may groom each other with their mouths. The young of all mammals suckle and by so doing form powerful bonds between mother and offspring. The letter to the Hebrews and the first letter of Peter use the analogy of new Christians being given spiritual milk. Similarly we human beings use our mouths as important communicators of relationship. Lovers 'taste' each other when they kiss: 'Let him kiss me with the kisses of his mouth! For your love is better than wine' says the Song of Songs (1:2). And so you can now buy flavoured cosmetics and edible clothing. Other relationships are sealed and confirmed with kisses – which is why Judas' kiss is such a terrible betrayal – kissing is the 'taste' of love, friendship and intimacy. Unsurprisingly that taste is typically described as 'sweet'.

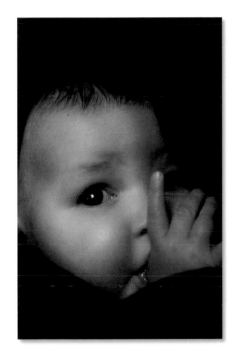

Both adults and children will often put their fingers in their mouths when anxious or in particular need of reassurance. Children often suck their thumbs. When another reassuring presence is not to hand, the body tastes itself and calls up a memory of the comforting Other. Similarly, like other animals we will often 'lick our wounds' and will suck at a painful scratch or burnt or bruised finger to heal the sense of breach and injury and to make the hurt go away. Our mouths then are powerful mediators of comfort, reassurance and relationship. Our mouths can suggest to us reconciliation and the beginning of healing.

Moving out: the taste of God

One of the ways in which we can begin to examine our spiritual journey as we move out from the foundations of Christian tradition is to look at the main taste sensations as metaphors for our relationship with God.

Sweet/Bitter

For example, the way God speaks to us is sometimes imagined as a form of feeding. God's word is delightful; so one way of imagining it is as a delicious and sweet taste:

> How sweet are your words to my taste,
> sweeter than honey to my mouth!
> Psalm 119:103

**O taste and see that
the Lord is good**
Psalm 34:8

Jeremiah also talks about 'eating' God's word and finding the experience delightful:

Your words were found, and I ate them,
And your words became to me a joy
And the delight of my heart;
For I am called by your name
Jeremiah 15:16

These images also remind us that when we encounter God's word with our whole heart and mind focused on it, it enters into us and becomes part of us – as though we had 'eaten' it. So God's word dwells within us and that relationship is the source of spiritual delight and joy.

However, God's word also carries with it responsibility. So when we are called to be prophetic witnesses, there may be bitterness along with the sweetness. For the prophets then, to be given God's word is ultimately sweet, but to deliver God's word to a people who have turned away is to experience bitterness. In these two examples, God's word is imagined as being written on a scroll that can be eaten:

> He said to me, Mortal eat this scroll that I give you and fill your stomach with it. Then I ate it; and in my mouth it was as sweet as honey
> Ezekiel 3:3

> 'Take it, and eat; it will be bitter to your stomach, but sweet as honey in your mouth.' So I took the little scroll from the hand of the angel and ate it; it was sweet as honey in my mouth, but when I had eaten it, my stomach was made bitter'
> Revelation 10:9–10

Consequently, when we share God's word with others, we are sharing an experience which is sweet and delightful; we offer people God's sweetness, so that they too may take it into themselves and be indwelt by the Word. At the same time, however, we are called to a prophetic witness which 'tastes bitter' because it must confront the injustice and suffering of the world with a call to repentance and to transformation. That bitterness is linked to emotions and feelings about the world, as we say in the phrase 'bitterly disappointed'.

Salt

Jesus knew all about food and drew people's attention to cooking, eating and hospitality to make them think about our lives before God. Salt, for example, had a particular significance for the people of his time. There was the importance of salt in the diet in a dehydrating climate; the importance of salt as a preservative and a symbolic use of salt in sacrifices and a way showing faithfulness. To eat bread and salt together was to make a bond of friendship and hospitality. So Jesus says:

Salt is good, but if salt has lost its saltiness, how can you season it? Have salt in yourselves. Mark 9:50

We are called to be salt, so people can 'taste' us in the mix of faiths and cultures within our society. That 'taste' carries the same obligations: to be salt in our society we should forge bonds of friendship and show our neighbour Christ's hospitality.

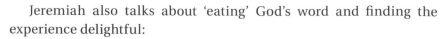

Sour

The image of 'sour grapes' which sets people's teeth on edge is used as a proverb in both Jeremiah 31:29–30 and in Ezekiel 18:2. That proverb provides an image of the 'sourness' of sin, which ruins the sweetness of the world and makes us recoil from the rottenness which has spoilt the Promised Land whose taste experience is 'milk and honey' (cf Exodus 3:8 etc).

So when God feeds his chosen people in the desert with manna, the experience of it is wonderfully sweet: 'the taste of it was like wafers made with honey' (Exodus 16:31), but when the Israelites tried to hoard it 'it bred worms and became foul' (Exodus 16:20). The relationship between human beings and God requires trust, obedience and right behaviour. When humans start deciding they know what is best, rottenness creeps in. In the feeding miracles, Jesus also refers people back to the manna experience and tells them (and us) clearly 'Do not work for the food that perishes, but the food that endures for eternal life, which the Son of Man will give you' (John 6:27).

In the original proverb about the 'sour grapes', the idea is that the sour taste of sin is communicated down the generations, but because of God's mercy, this no longer has to hold true. The sour taste of the brokenness of the world can be taken away, for God desires both reconciliation and healing for the creation and his intention is that human beings should experience the 'sweetness' of life. It is perhaps therefore an important detail in St John's account of the crucifixion, that Jesus should drink the 'sour wine' (John 19:29) and, having drunk it, should announce that 'It is finished'. Through Jesus, the world gone sour through human disobedience and destruction of God's sweetness, is redeemed.

Our task then in discovering our own spiritual journey, is to delight in, and to communicate the sweetness God intends for human life and for the whole creation. Yet this task also requires people to become aware of the sour taste in the heart of our society and become God's partners in restoring the sweetness.

Bitter

The bitter taste experience is used in a similar way in biblical imagery. Bitter herbs are an inherent part of the Passover meal, for example. The bitter herbs (typically eaten by Jews today as fresh grated horseradish) provoke memory and remind us to thank God for our lives and to count our blessings before we proceed to the feast prepared for us. This story sees the bitter herb not just as a reminder but as an image of all our human suffering and trials before the feast that God intends for us.

Think about a story

One of the well known stories of Rebbe Nachman of Breslov is of a Jew and a Gentile going to eat Passover with other Jewish families. The Gentile does not know what to expect, so is told to eat whatever he is given and to enjoy the marvellous feast. However, when the Gentile comes to eat he is given Matzos, salted cucumber and finally a pile of grated horseradish.

He is disgusted and runs out of the house. Complaining to his friend, he is reminded that he should have hung on just a little longer. First you eat the bitter herbs – *then* comes the feast.

The moral of the story is to remind us that as with Passover, so it is with life. But we often give up as soon as we reach the bitter part of life, forgetting that we are promised a real feast to look forward to. It is easy to get so bogged down in the difficult experiences that we forget to look forward with joy and hope.[1]

? In your spiritual journey, what bitter herbs have you encountered on the way?

Jesus' last supper would have included the same bitter herbs and that same reminder that God saves his people who come to the time of trial. Surely then, Jesus was reinforcing that message when he said 'Do this in memory of me' and urging his disciples to believe in the saving acts of God.

But we do not have to be passive observers and receivers of the bitterness of life. The saving acts of God for us in Jesus mean that Christians are required to look outward for the transformation of the world and to fight against injustice. If we do not, others will taste that bitterness:

Ah, you who call evil good and good evil,
who put darkness for light and light for darkness,
who put bitter for sweet and sweet for bitter!
Ah, you who are wise in your own eyes, and shrewd in your own sight!
Ah, you who are heroes in drinking wine and valiant at mixing drink,
who acquit the guilty for a bribe and deprive the innocent of their rights!
Therefore, as the tongue of fire devours the stubble,
and as dry grass sinks down in the flame,
so their root will become rotten, and their blossom go up like dust;
for they have rejected the instruction of the Lord of hosts,
and have despised the word of the Holy One of Israel.
Isaiah 5:20–4

This passage, which is full of taste and eating imagery, reminds us of our need to be indwelt by God's word, to experience its sweetness, to obey its requirements.

God's taste

Food sacrifices to God

Relationship between human beings and God has always acknowledged the importance of food. Food is the source of our life, energy and the sustenance of our bodies, so it makes sense to remember the Creator whenever we prepare food. Moreover, the animals and plants we eat have to die in order for us to consume them and their lives too, are to be remembered in the act of preparation and consumption. We should never eat as though food were just there for us to take as we will; it is always a gift and the act of tasting and eating it should remind us always that this gift comes from God.

In scripture then, we cannot overlook the spiritual significance of offerings made to God. Such offerings are deeply ingrained in the ancient rituals of many religions. The book of Leviticus lays down the rules for this inclusion of God and human beings in the food ritual. The sacrifice of food was made so that God could be included in 'tasting' it and 'smelling' the pleasing odour of the burnt offering. The shedding of precious life blood also came to carry the significance of atonement, the carrying away of sin, so that in the cathartic act of death and burning, right relationship between human beings and God could be affirmed. Human beings should therefore also not forget that God provides us with everything we have in creation and to give thanks for the life of the animals consumed. Scripture also makes it clear, that just giving God a cut of the spoil was never the point. Just offering a sacrifice or a burnt offering without turning the heart towards God in love and gratitude was a pointless waste.

O Lord, open my lips,
And my mouth will declare your praise.
For you have no delight in sacrifice;
If I were to give a burnt offering, you would not be pleased.
The sacrifice acceptable to God is a broken spirit
A broken and contrite heart,
O God, you will not despise.
Psalm 51:15–17

And even more directly, eating and being satisfied without thinking about justice for others not as fortunate as yourself would render the act of sacrifice not only pointless, but insulting to God:

What to me is the multitude of your sacrifices? Says the Lord;
I have had enough of burnt offerings of rams
And the fat of fed beasts
I do not delight in the blood of bulls,
Or of lambs, or of goats…

…Wash yourselves; make yourselves clean;
remove the evil of your doings
from before my eyes;
cease to do evil,
learn to do good;
seek justice, rescue the oppressed,
defend the orphan, plead for the widow
Isaiah 1:11;16–17

Eating and drinking then, intimately related to our bodies' needs, demands that we remember that every single human being on earth has such needs. Before we look to affirming our own right relationship with God, the act of tasting of food should remind us to give thanks that we can eat, and seek to do what we can to make sure that others can eat also.

Pause for prayer

God of corn and bread, of rice and chapatti,
we thank you for our food
and for the immense variety available to us.
We thank you for research that enables food to be grown
without destruction of the earth,
for developments that improve storage
so we waste less.
We pray for all who live and work
in rural communities,
for all who work the land
in this country and all over the world.
We pray for a more equal sharing
of the resources of the earth.
Lord, in your mercy
Hear our prayer [2]

If we meditate further on what relationship eating and drinking has to our own spiritual journey, we have to think about Jesus: first as God incarnate – 'the Son of Man came eating and drinking'; what he taught about food, his institution of the Eucharist at the Last Supper and his own sacrifice on the Cross.

Jesus as one who eats and drinks

The gospels give us a number of pictures of Jesus eating with people he has made his friends. Indeed, eating and drinking with them is a sign to all around that these are people with whom he is in relationship – and often occasioning scandal. Jesus is a person who seals friendships by accepting food, even if that food is offered by social outcasts and sinners. It is a picture of how it is really possible for people like us to entertain God in our lives. God's friendship towards us is signified by something that is possible for all of us, no matter how little we may have to share – the willingness to share is enough.

Moreover, those pictures of Jesus eating with his friends also offer us images of transformation at work: how God, when he comes into our lives, effects real change. In the encounter with Jesus, there is extraordinary saving change, which notwithstanding takes place in the ordinary world of sharing food. Zacchaeus, for example, offers to make restitution for his sins (Luke 19:8). When Jairus' daughter is restored, Jesus commands also that she be fed. After the resurrection, Jesus cooks his friends breakfast.

The feeding miracles

In John's gospel, the feeding of the five thousand is linked directly with Jesus' teaching about God. The miracle itself is brought about by using the 'five barley loaves and two fishes' – the food of the poor. Yet the act of sharing even so little generates an overabundance: God never stops giving where people share with one another. So, when yet more people turn up looking for bread, Jesus is able to make the point that has been so vigorously demonstrated: 'For the bread of God is that which comes down from heaven and gives life to the world' (John 6:33), 'I am the bread of life. Whoever comes to me will never be hungry, and whoever believes in me will never be thirsty' (John 6:35).

Eucharist

In the Eucharist feeding, sharing, indwelling God's word, 'tasting' Jesus by means of the bread of life, all come together. The sharing of food relates not just to bodily need but to the memory of God's deeds and desire for God's people to be saved and to be whole. Eating and drinking provokes prayer, praise and memory, so that human creatureliness is tied to God's intention. Moreover all the food and 'taste-experience' imagery of offering, sacrifice and bread of life, are gathered up in the Eucharist and focused on the gift of Christ's body and blood as our own particular feeding miracle expressed in fellowship and community. In the ordinary acts of eating and drinking, the congregation of God's people in right relationship with God is affirmed. But in terms of our spiritual journey, there is still the absolute conjunction of Eucharist with our duty to work for a peaceful, and just world. Eucharist offers us the chance to envision how God sees the world.

Prayer point

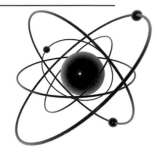

Eucharist is the feast of seeing behind and within,
behind the bread to the sales assistant,
baker, miller, farmer; to the plant, the seed,
the earth, to the sun and moon, air and water;
to the cosmic explosion that birthed the universe
to the God who is in all
and through all.

And also the knowledge that our eating starts another
process that leads back to the earth and
the perpetual recycling of the atoms,
temporarily part and parcel of this bread,
this particular part of the body of Christ.

Indeed the divine that is in this bread is sign and symbol
of the sacred process of recycling.[3]

Amen

Journey beyond tasting: inability to taste

Illness brings home to us how the inability to eat or taste speaks powerfully of loss of wholeness and how we need to be healed. People who are ill will lose their appetite or develop debilitating mouth disorders as a result of treatment. Not being able properly to use our mouths makes us feel especially cut off from the world.

The late John Diamond, in his book about his tongue cancer, *C,* writes about the tremendous debilitating effect not being able to eat or taste had on him – the more poignant and ironic perhaps because he was married to the celebrity cook Nigella Lawson. Rather than enjoy good food cooked by his wife he became angrier and angrier at being kept in hospital being fed through a tube.

> **Jevity** [the liquid nourishment he was fed through the nose] **comes in half-litre bottles, is beige in the way that old ladies' knickers in Fenwick's are beige, and is 500 malodorous calories' worth of assorted fats, fibres, proteins, triglycerides, vitamins and other life-sustaining oddments.**[4]

Eating is a great deal more than simply taking nourishment and losing the ability (rather than simply the desire) to eat became a symbol, for John Diamond, of his fight against cancer.

> **Before I was forced to think about it I'd assumed you put the food in your mouth, chewed it about a bit, swallowed, moved on to the peas. It turns out that unless you have a fully functioning tongue shovelling the stuff back towards the gullet as it passes through the scything teeth, the food just stays there at the front of your mouth, or worse, starts leaking back in the direction of your plate...**
>
> **...I tried some venison stew of which I managed that part of a single mouthful which didn't fall into the glass of Murphy's as I was trying to swig it down. That the rest of the stew finished up on the floor was through no fault of my tongue and entirely down to one of the rages I go into from time to time when not being me gets a little too much to bear.**
>
> **And so tonight I tried a small, soft pear.**
>
> **Same thing: chew, chew, dribble. The pear was about to go the way of the stew when I thought damn this thing and made it go down my throat. It wasn't exactly Robert the Bruce, but I jumped a little and ran to tell everyone that I'd eaten a pear...**[5]

Being able to eat again becomes a symbol of healing, the determination to live. This makes sense. When the body knows it is dying, people stop eating altogether. Eating and the celebration of life go together. So when people can no longer taste and cannot eat properly, this is an issue which should affect all of us who care about God's world and the people in it.

Reflecct on those who cannot taste

Veronica cannot taste anything today. She hasn't done for months. Veronica is suffering from several of the opportunistic infections which are part of living, and dying, with AIDS. She sits on the floor in her stone cottage, 12' x 10' with its rusty corrugated iron roof. Today two volunteer home-based carers, organised by the local Christian community, bring her some oil for her rough skin, some painkillers, and some meal for food. But although she eats a little, she cannot taste it. Her mouth is full of sores. She is aged 38 with five children.

Veronica probably does not have long to live. She will sit on that floor day after day until she dies, one of several million in sub-Saharan Africa, for whom the link between HIV/AIDS and poverty is all too real. Good food and clean water can help build up a person's immunity and keep the effects of being HIV positive at bay. Lack of food and unclean water all add to the spread of the virus. Poverty is increasing because AIDS is killing the 15–40 age range: the income-generating group. Poverty drives the men

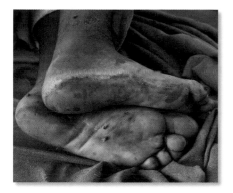

from the fields, because trade regulations mean that they cannot make a living from the soil, and into the urban centres where sexual faithfulness is harder. Poverty drives the young girls onto the streets to become sex workers. 'Who are all these new uncles?' says the youngster. 'If you want to eat tonight, we need all these uncles' replies the older sister. So the virus spreads.

In Zambia the debt to the World Bank is currently 7 billion dollars. There is no money for anti-retroviral medication; nor for clinics to ensure that its use is monitored properly; nor transport to get Veronica to a clinic. Her lack of taste is part of a huge question in which health, education, poverty, trade and debt are all aspects of the picture. 'Give us this day our daily bread' includes Veronica in our prayer, but it also includes all those agencies which are seeking to encourage young people to work for an AIDS free generation; encourage the empowerment of women to make their own sexual choices responsibly; encourage men to live faithfully and responsibly; make available proper use of condoms; encourage availability of nourishing food and clean water; engage national and global politics and economics in the implications of trade laws and the burden of debt on a nation's health and its future. No one can say that AIDS is not their problem – not to their taste. Veronica's lack of taste involves us all.

The double spiral: what do others taste?

The culture of food

In Redmond O'Hanlon's accounts of his travels among the indigenous peoples of Borneo and the Amazon, he gives detailed accounts of the things he has to eat and drink, including tapirs, peccaries and the eyes of spider monkeys. Mostly however, he shares with his companions the small staple fare which is their usual diet: rice or manioc. On each occasion, he takes a companion from England whose attitude to the food, O'Hanlon notes. In Borneo, the poet James Fenton exclaims with delight over a special treat of spaghetti, only to be told by O'Hanlon, that the treat is (literally) a can of worms. Fenton loses his lunch. (In reality show ordeals, eating such 'disgusting' food becomes entertainment for people who will never be hungry or need to eat such things in order to survive.) However, and perhaps more interestingly, his companion Simon, in South America, appalled by the poverty of the guides, finally flips and tells O'Hanlon he is getting out and going home:

'What will you do,' I said, suddenly envious, 'when you get home?'

'I will drink top-class wine,' said Simon, 'in huge quantities…we'll have pork and beef, on alternate Sundays, for family lunch. But I'll always do the potatoes because Liz never gets them quite crispy enough. Just round the edges, know what I mean?'[6]

Later, with Simon gone, when the guides have managed to kill a wild peccary, Simon's words come back to O'Hanlon.

'Wouldn't it be wonderful,' I said, 'to have it with apple sauce and gravy and crackling and roast potatoes…?'

'They boil it all – you'll see,' said Juan. 'It is the best way. Nothing is lost. The fat stays in the soup and not in the air. Roasting, Redmond, is for rich people'.[7]

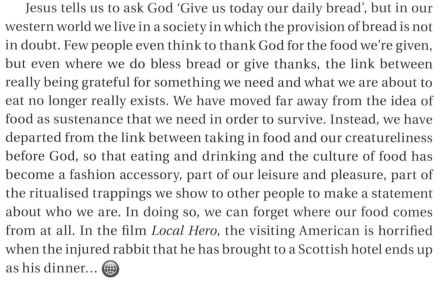

Jesus tells us to ask God 'Give us today our daily bread', but in our western world we live in a society in which the provision of bread is not in doubt. Few people even think to thank God for the food we're given, but even where we do bless bread or give thanks, the link between really being grateful for something we need and what we are about to eat no longer really exists. We have moved far away from the idea of food as sustenance that we need in order to survive. Instead, we have departed from the link between taking in food and our creatureliness before God, so that eating and drinking and the culture of food has become a fashion accessory, part of our leisure and pleasure, part of the ritualised trappings we show to other people to make a statement about who we are. In doing so, we can forget where our food comes from at all. In the film *Local Hero*, the visiting American is horrified when the injured rabbit that he has brought to a Scottish hotel ends up as his dinner...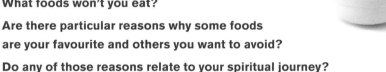

Think about food

What are your favourite foods?

What foods won't you eat?

Are there particular reasons why some foods are your favourite and others you want to avoid?

Do any of those reasons relate to your spiritual journey?

Eating out

> 'Everything we ate was competently executed and reasonably priced... Some things were better than we expected, like my pumpkin gnocchi with Parmesan and sage butter. Initially, these seemed bland, but with each mouthful I found myself warming to their nutty, buttery subtlety; it was with some surprise that I realised that my plate was empty....
>
> Our meal was mostly fine and dandy, we felt comfortable in the surroundings, there was plenty of eye candy of both sexes and we were treated extremely well. Our bill, with wine, was around £60. What's not to like?'[8]

This restaurant review demonstrates how distant the link is between our bodily needs and the culture of food in our western society. Eating out requires more than just the food on the plate, the restaurant has to give the diner an all round experience which involves aesthetic pleasure, the thrill of seeing beautiful people or celebrities, pampering by the staff and stimulation from original ways of preparing and presenting food. In some restaurants there is an inverse correlation between the miniscule portion of artistically prepared food with its lovely shapes and colours, and the price of the dish. Restaurant dining often has nothing whatsoever to do with being hungry or needing to eat – indeed many restaurants offer food for dieters who are trying *not* to eat – a trend mocked by one American diner which displayed a big notice: 'Margi's diner welcomes dieters – just ask and we provide half the food, and half the calories – full price'.

Visit an eating place

Next time you eat out at a restaurant, pub or café, write or talk through a review of what you ate.

What was good about the eating experience?

What was bad about the eating experience?

Would you recommend that experience to another would-be restaurant goer?

If not, what eatery would you recommend and why?

Is this exercise easier than recommending your faith? If so, why?

. . . .

The cult of the celebrity chef

The rituals of eating and drinking in western society manifest themselves in various ways. Eating out, where you pay money for someone else to produce the food is one such ritual, but equally, cooking at home and inviting others for dinner has acquired its own set of style gurus. Nigella Lawson will share with us what it takes to become a domestic goddess, for indeed, cooking and eating have become part of our people's self-defined spirituality. Television gives us all the clues we need: Delia Smith, Anthony Worrall-Thompson, Ainsley Harriott, Gary Rhodes, and Rick Stein are the merest soupçon in the plethora of celebrity chefs vying for our attention and allegiance as they take us gently through boiling eggs and steaming fish. Cooking is a science, as well as being an art, and we must master the science in order to move to the higher levels of artistic appreciation. If you don't appreciate it quite enough, Gordon Ramsay will come steaming out of his kitchen to put you right. It is a nice piece of irony perhaps, that the people's cook, Jamie Oliver, takes underprivileged youngsters and trains them to become *chefs* – producing food for people for whom money is no object – even though in today's society, chefs, like hairdressers, can become very high earners, and with a TV series, millionaires.

In the cult of the celebrity chef, we must concentrate on getting things exactly right so that the taste experience will be as exquisite as possible. We know what Jesus says about salt – but he had not met Delia.

In Delia Smith's book *Delia's How to Cook* (Book 2) there is a marvellous passage which illustrates so many of the things that we crave in our society.[9] First, we can elevate our common or garden salt to something rare and specific. She tells us that the very best salt for cooking is English sea salt from Maldon in Essex. Maldon salt only comes from Maldon – it has a name and a provenance. It is 'pure'. She tells us how the salt appeals to our senses in a particular way – it looks 'pretty', it crushes delightfully between the fingers, it tastes of the sea, and you can imagine the sound of it crunching through the salt mill. It figures in the exciting new experiences you can get from eating out and trying new things; it figures in innovation and new heights of pleasure. This is surely the only salt we can ever want or use. Delia tells us that if you wrap a chip in a rocket leaf, dip it in mayonnaise and Maldon salt, the taste experience is out of this world. But we must use it sparingly,

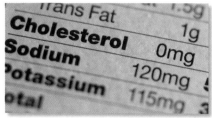

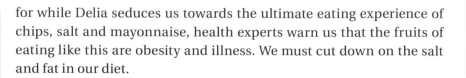

for while Delia seduces us towards the ultimate eating experience of chips, salt and mayonnaise, health experts warn us that the fruits of eating like this are obesity and illness. We must cut down on the salt and fat in our diet.

Eating and health

With such an emphasis on eating as part of the process which tells others who we are, it is no wonder that food becomes allied with our spiritual pathway. We no longer need to eat to stave off hunger, so people start to think about how what they put in their bodies affects their holistic sense of themselves as 'spiritual' people. 'Purity' is an important concept; impurities must be purged. Drinking 'pure' mineral water becomes an art itself and a little bottle of water a fashion accessory. Coca Cola had to withdraw its own bottled water *Dasani*, when it was revealed to be purified tap water with some taste elements put back in. Really pure water, just doesn't 'taste' right – a deeply ironic idea when you think of the millions of people for whom clean water would be the difference between life and death.

None of us in our society is likely to die from our drinking water, yet the spiritual journey often contains many practices and therapies for 'detoxification'. If you eat and drink too much of the 'wrong' sort of food over Christmas, then you must start the New Year with programmes for flushing the toxins out of your body, losing weight and feeling better. Although once Christians fasted before the feast, the process is now turned around. Bingeing is followed by fasting, the guilt of overeating by spiritual wellbeing. You can go to a health 'farm', there to be restored to your true and beautiful nature. This is quite different to the ancient religious traditions of fasting, where the intention is to stop being complacent about provision, to think of the needs of others and to focus the mind on God. Jesus made this quite clear during his own fasting experience: 'One does not live by bread alone, but by every word that comes from the mouth of God' (Matthew 4:4).

Obesity, eating disorder and dieting

People in our society are therefore caught up in a terrible tension between eating food they don't need and guilt about the results of eating it which interfere with the need to look good and keep pure. It is a war between the pursuit of pleasure as part of your right to make choices, and the consequences of those choices. Jesus' point about the natural process of consuming food and disposing of the waste products (Mark 7:18) and the defilement which comes from corrupt human behaviour is particularly sharp in this context. In general, the war is being lost as people become increasingly obese – the amount of food consumed no longer relates to the amount of energy people need to go about their daily lives. (See the film *Super Size Me*, and Morgan Spurlock's experiment of eating nothing but McDonald's food.)[10] The British government is seriously worried about the obesity of the population and the strain this puts on health resources, as people eat themselves into illness. We are also victims of food manipulation. What we like to taste is not necessarily good for us – as Winnie the Pooh found out when he ate too much honey at Rabbit's house and got stuck in the hole on the way

out. Chemicals can make our food more attractive and possibly more dangerously seductive: 'alcopops' for example. Further, a combination of technology and strategic importing can offer us our favourite foods all year round instead of at the appropriate time and season.

For the writer and philosopher Jean-Paul Sartre, in *Nausea* the sense of alienation from society fills Antoine Roquentin with a sense of pointlessness and absurdity and drags our attention back to the question: what do we eat and drink *for*? His own reaction is to be filled with the Nausea –both a physical need to vomit and the sense of spiritual emptying out and loss. This emptiness is seen in people around us where overeating and emptying are symptoms of a profound loss of self-identity and confidence in the essential goodness of the self.

So in some people, the amount we eat generates body-image anxieties and in extreme cases leads to eating disorders such as anorexia nervosa and bulimia. Here the relation between food and bodily need is destroyed altogether as anorexics may chew food but refuse to swallow it; bulimics eat the food and then regurgitate it. Interfering with the body's ability to absorb food, similarly, treats some compulsive eaters. Diets that purport to achieve weight loss without losing the pleasure of eating sell millions and are cheerfully endorsed by celebrities. There are now 'Atkins' restaurants in which every last carbohydrate has been tracked down and destroyed. We are much more concerned with the effects of food *on* our bodies, than the simple human use of food *by* our bodies. This spills over into the way we treat animals, so that dog and cat lovers can give their pets different menus with a variety of smells and added ingredients, which are supposed to better health and add entertainment to the pets' dining experience.

So it is that people's spirituality may dictate that certain sorts of food must be consumed to ward off disease. People may employ nutritionists as just another kind of style guru or personal trainer. We are what we eat and we so easily fall victim to the education of our desire. But people who review their eating habits and decide they want to eat healthily, and in consciousness of what our bodies really need, demonstrate conclusively that it is possible to change.

'So when the woman saw that the tree was good for food, and that it was a delight to the eyes and that the tree was to be desired to make one wise, she took of its fruit and ate; and she also gave some to her husband, who was with her and he ate'
Genesis 3:6

Guarantees
a **better deal**
for Third World
Producers

FAIRTRADE

Abuse of taste

The story of the Fall reminds us that there are some pleasures we just should not taste. Pursuit of pleasure can lead us into sin: actions which hurt other people whether we mean them to or not. We have to learn self-denial, obedience and imagine the consequences of our decisions. If we are not sure what is the right thing to do, then we should listen to God who, as our loving Father, will not give us stones when we ask for bread. Similarly, God also reminds us that there are some things we should not meddle with or think we can just take as of right. The story of the Fall requires us to think about the way we eat and drink in our own society; whether we ever stop to think where our food comes from and who was responsible for making it available to us. There are ethical issues of justice involved with the decisions to buy certain kinds of food. Abuse of taste happens when we buy food that has been produced by means of exploitation of our fellow human beings. Our acts of eating and drinking reflect what we think of our global community and our care for God's people.

Feeding the hungry

So, if we are to engage in effective witness, we must not only understand ourselves as human creatures, but think properly about our attitudes to global hunger. Christians are good at thinking about people who are starving and raising money for famine relief. We respond often by (literally) throwing food at people. But do we ever bother to spend any time learning about food and 'eating' from people who really are starving? Does it make sense to raise money for the hungry at a church event and then go home and roast our dinner and throw the scraps away? What have we learned about God's desire to feed the hungry? We often pay little attention to the feeding miracles of Jesus or indeed Jesus' rebuke to the disciples in Matthew 16. Such stories contain much to remind us about producing food in a way that is directly related to the feeding needs of a community. In our supermarket culture, we have lost this reciprocity and indeed exploited food so shamelessly that even those who do know what they should grow can no longer afford to do so. This means people whose feeding cycle was well established go hungry while non-consumable cash crops blow in the wind around them. As Jesus says, who would give their child a stone or a snake when they ask for bread or fish (cf Matthew 7:10) – it doesn't make sense – but this is just the position we have put many poor countries in.

Investigate your food

Have a look through your cupboard or your fridge and take out a few items. Make a list of the countries of origin.

What issues do these countries face?

Think about who produced the food. Do you know if it was fairly traded?

How much do you know about food producers in these countries?

What would it take to find out?

When you cook or eat these items, remember to pray for those who grew or produced the food in the first place.
. . . .

Greed

Abuse of the gift of taste also includes greed. Greed begins from the idea of eating exclusively for oneself and refusing to share what we have with others. So greed also extends into all selfish behaviour which refuses to acknowledge the needs of others. In William Golding's *Pincher Martin*, the main character, Christopher, comes to realise that his whole life has been dictated by greed, relentlessly pursuing his own selfish desires. He sees his life imagined as a series of maggots in a tin box. The maggots eat each other until there is only one huge surviving maggot. He is the surviving maggot, but what will he turn into? Because he only knows how to survive, he forgets the place of God in his life and so his greed propels him into a hell of his own making where acts of desperate eating make him sick and ill. Finally, God asks him 'have you had enough, Christopher?'

In an individualised and often desperately greedy and selfish society, the spiritual journeys of people do often lead them to answer this question in the affirmative. Many people simply have had enough. There is no more room in the tin box. Our task as Christians is to offer another way of living and being that treats the underlying illness of which the symptom is endless greed. There is a point for everyone when 'enough is enough'.

Obsessive eating

In the Monty Python film, *The Meaning of Life*, one of the most unforgettable characters is Mr Creosote. Mr Creosote is one of life's diners. Hugely and grotesquely fat, when he arrives at the restaurant the obsequious waiter offers him the richest and most select items on the menu. Mr Creosote says he'll have the lot, plus large amounts of wine and proceeds to be sick into a bucket. At the end of a scene of gorging and vomiting, Mr Creosote swears he is full and cannot eat another thing, but is tempted when the waiter offers him a last 'wafer thin mint'. Mr Creosote, driven by greed, eats it, and promptly explodes.

For some people in our society, eating has become the only way of coping with the stress and complexity of their lives. Like drugs, eating certain foods can become addictive and people will consume them until they become ill or even die. Typically people will say that they eat without even tasting the food – the physical sensation of eating is bypassed. As with drugs, people need liberating from this self-destructive behaviour. They need to be set free.

Comfort food

In one episode of *The Vicar of Dibley* Dawn French responds to being dumped by an unscrupulous lover by eating a fridge full of ice cream and a multitude of chocolate bars. She is too ashamed and unhappy to go to church to lead worship on Sunday and finally resigns.

Her congregation refuse to accept her resignation and she is helped by pictures of an unborn baby and by the village putting out a banner saying 'we love you'

What does this tell us about food, faith, love and healing?

The spirals entwined: tasting with others

What is fasting?

Clearly, as Christians we must pay attention to our bodily human needs. We are made as creatures before God who cannot function or be healthy without adequate food. The question is, do we ever actually think about eating in any realistic way? Christians in the western world often give up chocolate or alcohol for Lent, but this is not *fasting*, it is not a discipline which asks us questions about what we really need, but mere deprivation of a pleasure or habit that makes the Easter egg and the glass of wine taste wonderful at the end and allows ourselves to feel good about ourselves in the process. What does it take to become conscious of what our body needs (and doesn't need) and what *else* does it take to use that new understanding of what it means to be human to focus on God's desire for us? Jesus' example of fasting in the wilderness saw him transforming the awareness of being hungry into a deeper and more profound relationship with God. The test of that activity was a temptation which allowed him to place the preciousness of that relationship before his desire for food. If we are properly to observe Lent, what are we going to take on to strengthen our walk with God? Sometimes others outside the Church, feel the power of Jesus' example more than we do.

The Holy Qu'ran's injunction to Muslims to fast during Ramadan (Sura II v185). One of the Five Pillars of Islam.

Reflection point

Some people were laughing at a nurse at a party. She was usually the first to have a few glasses of wine, but was drinking soft drinks. When asked why, she said she had given up alcohol for Lent.

> **'But you're not a Christian and you don't go to Church' said a friend.**
> **'I know,' said the nurse, 'but I still like to give up something for Lent.'**
> **'Why?' asked the friend.**
> **'Because Jesus did,' the nurse replied.**

Hospitality

Another important place where the spirals of our spiritual journey and that of others outside the Church entwine is within the tradition of hospitality. People of other faiths and none are often better than us at inviting people for meals and showing love and generosity. In scripture, hospitality towards friends and strangers is a direct witness of God's love. We must feed others in recognition of their humanity and to let them know we see and respond to their need. So it is that Abraham welcomes angels to his dining table. Hospitality in church is part of a ministry of welcome and of making strangers and friends feel at home. We need to think seriously about this, especially where Christian courses use meals to promote fellowship and as an invitation to faith. Is our hospitality just to be a Christians only affair, or can we really be hospitable towards our neighbours and people unlike ourselves? Many churches have a wide programme of social activities where people are invited to meals and parties, especially at Christmas, but what does it take to keep that hospitality available for people and to build on those relationships as Jesus did?

A cup of traditional green coffee (ghawa) with Turkish delight (raha haloum) and dates on a silver tray. Traditional Arab Ramadan fast-breaking treats.

Using taste: journeying into Christian tradition

Feasting

Professor David Ford writes:

> To have a vision of the Kingdom of God, and to want to have foretastes of it now, is therefore to be concerned for many things and people coming together. Perhaps the biggest vision of all is given in one verse of the Letter to the Ephesians which speaks of God having
>
> > A plan for the fullness of time, to gather up [unify, recapitulate, consummate] all things in Christ, things on heaven and things on Earth. (Ephesians 1.10)
>
> This is a stupendous picture of Jesus Christ as the host of the universe, entertaining everything and everyone. Let us stretch our imaginations to begin to conceive the significance of that. It of course embraces the literal hospitality...with feasting as the practice that can most clearly hint at the ultimate destiny to which God is inviting us. That in turn involves the healing of relationships, forgiveness of wrongs, justice, and all that makes for the sort of peace in which people can enjoy each other across their differences.[15]

You must sit down, sayes Love, and taste my meat: so I did sit and eat

George Herbert, *Love III*

When Jesus talks about the Kingdom, he does so in terms of a feast, to which all God's people are invited. The trouble with us is that we don't take the invitation seriously, we find other things to do, or we stick the invitation on the mantelpiece and forget to reply. We get distracted or occupy ourselves with other matters that we think are more important. Yet when we *do* remember, that feast is still there waiting for us. God's hospitality is endless and boundless and each of us is honoured guest. Like the prodigal son, it does not matter what we have done or what we deserve, as long as we return to the one who has never ceased searching for us.

Where have we been?

This chapter has asked us to think about the experience of taste and therefore also to think about how and what we eat and how we share food with others.

❖ We have a number of basic taste sensations, which contribute to the way we eat and enjoy food. We also use our mouths for intimacy and comfort and to affirm precious relationships.

❖ Some of the basic taste sensations appear in biblical imagery to teach us more about our relationship with God. God's word to us is 'sweet', but prophetic witness in society can be 'bitter' when we have to confront elements of that society which are contrary to God's will. Jesus calls us to be distinctive, to be as 'salt' in our communities and we should be aware of how sin corrupts God's sweetness in creation and turns it sour. Jesus redeems this sourness.

❖ The Bible also teaches us about the ancient rituals of sacrificial offerings and the importance of their symbols in understanding the relationship between human beings and God. We are called to seek justice and trans-formation, without that, food offerings have no meaning. As God incarn-ate, Jesus also shows us plainly the link between sharing food and right relationship; his example is supremely given to us in the Eucharist.

❖ Those who cannot taste are often ill. Illness, such as the HIV/AIDS pandemic, teaches us about the relationship between food and healing and our responsibility to work for that healing in God's world.

❖ In our western society, eating has become divorced from the physical needs of the body. Eating is about the selfish pursuit of pleasure and so we become occupied by the problems of eating – fighting fat, searching for purity, detoxifying ourselves after bingeing.

❖ The Bible warns us against eating the wrong thing, but we can still fall into abusing our sense of taste by giving into greed or obsessive reliance on food we can't even taste any more. Where this happens, we need to be set free. Our task is to feed the hungry, not eat ourselves to death.

❖ The example of fasting teaches us something about our physical need for food and our spiritual need for God. The traditions of hospitality allow us to witness to our love of neighbour and of God.

❖ The feast is a sign of the Kingdom and the hope of heaven. Everyone is invited. It is where our spiritual journey ends. Yet the story of the prodigal is also where many people outside the Church would also hope their spiral path to God will end.

Reflect on 1 Peter 2:1–3

Rid yourselves, therefore, of all malice, and all guile, insincerity, envy and all slander. Like newborn infants, long for the pure, spiritual milk, so that by it you may grow into salvation – if indeed you have tasted that the Lord is good.

> Each door from the room says,
> this is not all. Your hands will find
> in the dark.
>
> Archbishop Rowan Williams

Journey into Imagination

Starting the journey: what is imagination?

This is a somewhat different chapter, in which the sense journeys we have undertaken are pulled together in order to understand the creative worlds our minds are capable of, and how these creative worlds relate to our spiritual lives. The journey into imagination also allows our spiral journey to intersect with the visionaries and dreamers of the Christian tradition, who have helped us to think more deeply and imaginatively about God. All the information we receive from our senses tells us directly about our world and our place in it, but beyond this, we have mental worlds which are capable of using that information as a foundation for the imagination.

Within our own heads, we have the capacity to create and control stories of our own. We can construct, images, narratives, we can wonder and dream. Our mental world is not limited by our physical capabilities, nor by our physical location in space and time. Through acts of the imagination we can travel and journey to anywhere we want to go. The imagination opens doors in our mental worlds to all kinds of possibility, both good and bad, where we can explore who we are and test out what we want to be. Children unselfconsciously dramatise and act out the worlds of their imagination; as we age, we tend to lock up our imaginative experience and keep it to ourselves, unless it is released by means of hobbies, past-times, or giving ourselves permission to play with our children and grandchildren. Imagination can be stimulated by creative entertainment – books, TV programmes, films, computer and console games, and pop videos can all stimulate the imagination – although we need our critical faculties to separate out the gold from the dross. Imagination is the safe-keeper of our identity; people who are deprived of sensory stimulus, for example in extreme hostage situations, will call on the imagination and memory for the means to confirm who they are to themselves and in order to stay sane.

Imagine your desert island

Make a list of 10 things that would keep your mind active on a tiny desert island. Choose favourite books, films, music or games.

Why are these special to you, or what's so good about them?

Our imagination needs to be fed. We need experiences which are fed into memory, reflected on and then added to as we call them up and examine them or incorporate them with other elements. We need ideas which stimulate the imagination and provoke our mental faculties to speculate, analyse, wonder and dream. We need emotional responses which colour and shape what our imagination does. Walter

Brueggemann writes about the 'prophetic imagination' – the way the prophets were able to bring God's word to bear imaginatively on Israel's situation and by that means confront the people with the need to change and conform to God's will.

Our imaginations enable us to explore hypothetical situations, 'what if?' scenarios, but that does not mean that acts of imagination only deal with fictions or dreams, like what our life would be like if we won the lottery (best case scenario?) or our loved one was run over (worst case scenario). Acts of imagination can also reveal the truth of situations more clearly. If, after a blazing row you revisit in your imagination what was said and done, you can usually see more clearly what the problems were and what now needs to be done to heal the rift. Or, in other cases, you may need imagination to allow you to remove your rose-tinted spectacles and see some situations are not all they appear. Imagination offers us bounded possibilities of creativity and enjoyment, but used with our critical faculties, imagination is a gift that ties us more clearly to an understanding of the world and our place in it.

Our imagination also plays an important part in our response to God and in the way we walk our spiritual journey. The way we read scripture, the way we worship, the way we pray and reflect – all these things are subject to our imagination acting on our experience of the Christian faith. It should not be surprising to us that more and more people are today experiencing God in dreams, in mental images and reflections and within imaginative exploration of some other spiritual pathway. Further, people are also using their imaginations to explore the spiritual and to set it against what they understand as the traditional hold the Church has had on images and ideas of God. In many cases, those acts of imagination are understood by Christians as hostile witnesses to our faith. But is that really the case?

Stop reading and allow yourself two 15-minute daydreams

First, imagine the best possible scenario you can think of, no matter how self-indulgent. A holiday? More money? Freedom from illness? All your stress and worries being magically solved? Let your imagination go where it likes, no matter how impossible and improbable.

Secondly, imagine your worst nightmare. The death of a loved one? A time of pain and suffering? A war? A divorce? Being charged with a crime? Imagine fully the emotional quality of this scenario. What are its consequences and how do you see yourself within it?

Moving out: imagining God in our time

Dreams

The dream is the small hidden door in the deepest and most intimate sanctum of the soul

Carl Gustav Jung, *The Meaning of Psychology for Modern Man*, 1934

The dream is the small hidden door in the deepest and most intimate sanctum of the soul

Carl Gustav Jung, *The Meaning of Psychology for Modern Man*, 1934

Scripture tells us a great deal about the way God can move within our minds and hearts. In the world of the bible, dreams and visions are part of the stuff of spiritual life, but others may have to sort out what the dreams 'mean'. Because imagination is so powerful and so wide-ranging, we may sometimes need help to sort out what is going on in our heads. In bookshops today, we can sometimes find books or 'dictionaries' on dream or vision interpretation which offer particular correspondences between dream images and what you are really supposed to be exploring. For example:

To dream that your eyelashes are growing, signifies that good health and fortunes will be with you.
http://www.dreammoods.com/dreamthemes/bodyparts.htm

Fun though they may be, these crude tools unfortunately add very little to our understanding of the imagination at work. Indeed, the development of psychoanalytic technique and spiritual direction in our own times has demonstrated the need for much more complex and empathic relationships in dealing with people's imaginative worlds. Sharing and talking about such experiences requires careful analysis of psychological implications, symbolic structures and the personal mythology and interpretative capability of the dreamer. And, quite simply, you might dream about your eyelashes because you have a fallen one sticking in your eye.

Scripture, however, makes it clear that the way we deal with acts of imagination has to be more complex and sensitive than this. For example, in Genesis 40:25ff, Joseph talks to Pharaoh about the troubling dreams he has been having.* First, Joseph contextualises the dream by indicating that Pharaoh is imagining a future which is under the sovereignty of God. His imagination reaches out to that future in terms of his responsibilities towards his people and their welfare. He must determine right action in response to the promptings of his imagination.

***It is just as well Joseph did not have access to the dreammoods website where 'to see a cow with a skeleton face, suggests that your mother or motherly figure in your waking life is displaying a lack of emotions. She is being unresponsive to your needs' and 'To see a herd of cows, indicates your need to belong'. There are, however, those practising Christian interpretation by means of biblical models, such as John Paul Jackson in the USA.**

Our imaginative acts, dreams and wondering have the facility of calling our attention to situations we must resolve, decisions we must make and actions we must take.[4] Joseph (Matthew 2:13) is warned in a dream about the danger to Jesus and so changes his travel plans; Peter's dream (Acts 10:11) opens up access to the world of the gentiles (Acts 10:45; Acts 11:1–18).

This is not simply a matter of reacting to evil omens and portents or the employment of psychic powers. Actions which point to salvation come about from creative imaginative engagement with situations and environments in which we seek to discover what God intends for us. Moreover apocalyptic writing, as in the book of Revelation, shows the immersion of a Christian imagination in searching for, and finding, a vision of God's intention and purpose for our future.

We have to engage seriously with the world of sleep-dreams and day-dreaming, because an increasing number of people believe that God has spoken to them in dreams and some people of other faiths have converted to Christianity following dreams about Jesus. What are we to make of this phenomenon and how far do we understand the role and function of dreaming in our own lives? *Healing Dreams* (Triangle 1993) and *Dream Stories* (BRF 2002) by Russ Parker include an examination of how God has spoken to his people in dreams and continues to do so today. How do we walk with people who are dogged by nightmares, and reach past the dreamcatchers to understand and relieve their pain?

Feelings and emotions

A number of studies have shown that people today increasingly are willing to admit to spiritual experiences which often begin with a physical sensation which is then read in imagination as having significance beyond that person's experience of the 'ordinary' physical world. For example, in David Hay and Kate Hunt's work *Understanding the Spirituality of people who don't go to Church*, they cite the case of 'Tom' whose experiences included leading ghost hunts and sensing 'atmospheres' in people's houses.[1] Yet when Tom was waiting in hospital for news of his seriously ill father he experienced 'a sudden rush of warmth and a sense that someone was telling him not to worry, that everything was going to be all right'. This was an experience quite *opposite* to the cold and spooky world of ghosts and 'atmospheres', a quality of hope and optimism overlaid on Tom's feelings of anxiety and unknowing. Significantly, Tom kept this experience to himself, locked away within his imagination and memory. One of our important tasks in moving out along the double spiral of our spiritual life is to find appropriate ways of releasing these experiences and affirming the movement of God in people's lives.

Stories and parables, hermeneutics

Jesus was also aware of the power and importance of imagination and urged those who came to hear him to use the gift of imagination to focus more clearly on God. In the parables, for instance, Jesus tells stories, but stories which take the daily experiences of people and draw out new forms of imagining. For example, in the parable of the labourers in the vineyard (Matthew 20:1 16), listeners are required imaginatively to enter into the lives of the first labourers and to empathise emotionally with their dismay when their labour has no more reward than the last to be hired. This empathic and imaginative response is required, otherwise the point Jesus wants to make about equality and God's justice will not be transforming of minds and hearts. There is a confrontational element to the narrative which requires the commitment of imagination, not just uncritical acceptance. Similarly, the parable of the prodigal son (Luke 15:11–32) includes the brother's outraged reaction and the parable of the Good Samaritan (Luke 10:30–7) carries the shocking revelation that the hurt man's 'neighbour' is his hated enemy.

Worship and imagination

The writer and artist David Jones once wrote that in worship you could think of a million and one things in the time it takes for the priest to pass from the epistle to the gospel side of the altar. By this he did not mean that you can sink into a little daydream (though that can happen...), but that participation in worship incites our imagination to focus more deeply on God's world and our part within it. Because the Eucharist

includes *anamnesis*, a making present of the past in expectation of the future, so acts of worship open up our imagination both to history and to the hope of heaven. In his writings, David Jones tried to show that creative writing is also like that, imagining new narrative is also a form of *anamnesis* and as such is irrevocably related to the creative acts of God. So, in his long poem *The Sleeping Lord* David Jones imagines a Eucharist in which the priest reaches that part of the Roman Catholic liturgy when he recalls to mind all those who have died. In the poem, that memory branches out to all those other Christians who have worshipped God before this present time, in all kinds of different situations. His memory extends further into the rites and ceremonies of pre-Christian times, finding echoes of Christ and Eucharist even here and thinking of people unknown and long gone yet who are still loved and longed for by God. In that short space of time, he holds up a vision of the way we all belong to one another in the Body of Christ, until his vision encompasses 'the departed/of the entire universal orbis/from the unknown beginnings/unguessed millenniums back/until now:/ FOR THESE ALL/he makes his silent, secret/devout and swift memento'.[2] David Jones himself derived a great deal of inspiration for his poetry and painting from worship and the cycle of prayer within a religious community. The discipline of that life of prayer allowed his imagination to develop and to flourish.

Worship then, should be the enabler, not the stifler of our spiritual imagination. This requires to think more carefully about what good worship is, since truly creative worship opens up our imaginative response but worship which is merely superficially attractive or entertaining has the capacity to distract us and actually prevent us from furthering our spiritual journey.

Many Christians enjoy the worship traditions within some expressions of Celtic spirituality[3] or enjoy Taizé worship, for the capacity they have to allow the imagination to soar.

A prayer of St Patrick

May the strength of God pilot us.
May the power of God, preserve us.
May the wisdom of God, instruct us.
May the hand of God protect us
May the way of God direct us.
May the shield of God defend us.

May the host of God guard us
against the snares of evil
and the temptations of the world.

May Christ be with us.
Christ before us.
Christ in us.
Christ over us.
May Thy salvation, O Lord,
be always ours
this day and forever more.
Amen

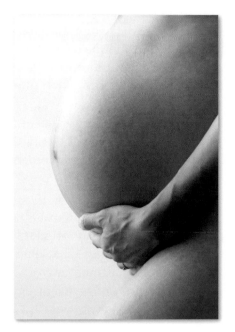

New imaginings about God, the mystical tradition

One of the wonderful things about the Christian tradition that we draw on is the imaginative response of other Christians who have left us their own dreams, wondering and visions about what it means to walk with God. In her *Revelations of Divine Love*, for example, Julian of Norwich (1342–*c*.1416) leaves us images of God as mother as well as father, expanding our imaginative capacity for exploring and wondering at the nature of God and our spiritual journey in relationship with God. By means of this imaginative exploration of God's nature, we may find ourselves better equipped to explore and share faith with those who have difficulty with, say, exclusive images of God as Father.

Or, for example, St John Chrysostom (347–407) has left us his nineteenth homily which is a commentary on the Lord's Prayer. In this, we are asked to shut the doors of the mind so that we cannot be distracted and to send our imagination towards God in heaven. In purifying (not destroying) our passions we can make this very earth a heaven for ourselves and others, and through gentleness and forgiving others we become more like the Father.[4]

For further inspiration on the modern spiritual search in relation to the wisdom of the Fathers and Mothers of the Church, see for example, Rowan Williams, *Silence and Honey Cakes*, Lion publishing 2003.

Divine Love

It is God's will that we have three things in our seeking:

The first is that we seek earnestly and diligently, without sloth, and, as it may be through His grace, without unreasonable heaviness and vain sorrow.

The second is, that we abide Him steadfastly for His love, without murmuring and striving against Him, to our life's end: for it shall last but awhile.

The third is that we trust in Him mightily of full assured faith. For it is His will that we know that He shall appear suddenly and blissfully to all that love Him.

Julian of Norwich, *Revelations of Divine Love*, chapter 10

The imagination of God

When we move out into the spiral of our spiritual journey and use our minds and bodies to encounter God's world, it is worth reminding ourselves that everywhere we meet the fruits of God's own imagination. Thinking about God as the imaginer of all things in the act of creation, allows us to begin to explore 'the mind of God'. In the book of Job (ch 38ff) there is an exposition of God's creative power, leading Job into the whole mystery of the creation within which the breadth of God's imagination is revealed. The creation is the ever changing world of God's imagining and is available to us not just as the experience of our world now, but in what we know of the past and what we can guess of the future.

Consequently, when we learn about the history of human culture, the geological past of our world with its many ages of biodiversity and the maths and physics of the early universe, we are not just accruing more knowledge but being given more insight into God's imagination. So we should not assume that knowledge of God is only confined to the

disciplines of theology and philosophy, because these are only part of the exploration of the places God is. The world of mathematics for example, seems extraordinarily complex and abstract to non-mathematicians, but many people who are gifted in this discipline have found that the study enriches their understanding of God and causes them to be amazed with wonder at the richness provided by research into their discipline. So in order to understand the imagination of God, we need to learn as much as we can of each other in community because this enables links to be made across knowledge disciplines and to find connections and bridges where the Holy Spirit has inspired women and men to join up new areas of thought and understanding.

This does not mean we have to become academic experts in all kinds of different branches of knowledge, but it does remind us to be open to different kinds of learning experience. Joining an art class, learning how to do basic DIY, reading popular history or science books, all of these things can open up worlds for our imagination to work on. There is a tremendous variety of material on the television and on the internet for us to journey into and discover more of God's works among us.

Psalm 111:2–7;10

Great are the works of the Lord,
studied by all who delight in them.
Full of honour and majesty is his work,
and his righteousness endures forever.
He has gained renown by his wonderful deeds;
the Lord is gracious and merciful.
He provides food for those who fear him;
he is ever mindful of his covenant.
He has shown his people the power of his works
in giving them the heritage of the nations.
The works of his hands are faithful and just;
all his precepts are trustworthy.

The fear of the Lord is the beginning of wisdom.

Beyond imagination: mental illness

We may realise what a tremendous gift our imaginations are, when we encounter people whose mental worlds are damaged, uncontrolled, distorted or destroyed. We need to understand what happens to the lives of people suffering from mental illness such as schizophrenia or psychosis and to the lives of people who have sought mental expansion or euphoria inside mind altering drugs, but who have then fallen prey to addiction and the mental hell that that entails.[10] Many of us will encounter people among our family and friends who fall victim to Alzheimer's disease or to other kinds of memory loss and dementia.

Have a look at *Iris*

This film, starring Kate Winslet, Judi Dench and Jim Broadbent, is based on the lives of Iris Murdoch and John Bayley as they coped with Iris' Alzheimer's disease.

Mental illness either distorts and fragments the imagination so that its coherence is lost and its actions are painful and frightening, or the imagination is lost altogether so that the person searches for who they are or simply becomes 'dead' and cold, like a light gone out.

The gospels tell us that Jesus was particularly moved by people with mental illness and that his healing ministry included helping those people to recover their 'right mind' as in the case of the Gerasene demoniac. Mental illness requires sensitive and careful assessment and treatment but Christian prayer and support can be absolutely essential in hearing what God still wants of people with such illness. Particularly sensitive listening is required, because people who are mentally ill may have difficulty communicating their spiritual needs and insights, but that does not mean that they do not have real and significant stories of God to tell and share. Including people who are mentally ill within the fellowship of spiritual wayfarers means that we must summon up all of our own imaginative engagement in order to allow those people to trust us with their stories, to find in us a means to cohesiveness and a path through confusion and mental darkness. Here, for example, is a story of depression:

> I am having a hard time writing what I'm feeling – even while writing this, I feel that my story is 'not good enough' – but I want people to know that this feeling is a symptom of your depression, and that it is not your fault.
>
> I struggle daily with self-acceptance, trying to see myself as bright, pretty and kind. Often, I see the opposite – dumb, ugly and mean. The energy that I spend trying to feel 'normal' is huge, but it is what I want more than anything in the world – to be mentally healthy and emotionally stable.[5]

For many people all their available energy goes into imagining themselves as people worthy of stepping outside and taking part in society. When imagination fails, they see themselves as worthless, hopeless, pointless and may try to harm themselves or commit suicide. Our spiritual journey carries with it a duty to help such people in our lives and communities around us by re-imagining them as the people God wants them to be, the people represented by Jesus' healing actions.

The Samaritans and other supporters

Find out about 'Extreme Listening' or find out about another agency helping people with mental illness, such as MIND. What could you do to help or support people in your own family or community?

The double spiral: what do others imagine?

There is evidence all around us in our society of people using the power of imagination and there is evidence too of exploration of the spiritual journey in fiction, TV and film, in music, poetry and dance. That exploration however often leads people to see a conflict with the Church, which is perceived as having a stranglehold on the story of salvation in such as way as to prevent 'magical world' of wondering and dreaming from emerging and changing people's lives.

Fiction

Chocolat

In the novel *Chocolat*, by Joanne Harris, which was made into a very successful film, the main female character 'stands for' spirituality, while the repressive priest 'stands for' the Church. On one side of the street, the people of the village go to church during their Lenten fast, on the other side of the street, Vianne, the non churchgoing Pagan, full of life and love, opens up her chocolate shop full of alluring treats. Gradually, the villagers drift from one side to the other, entering the chocolate shop and receiving a more vital and complete kind of pastoral care. Vianne feeds them chocolates which speak to their needs, listens to their troubles, rescues people from their oppression and sets them free. In the end, the priest too crosses the street determined to smash up Vianne's Pagan festival at Easter, but succumbs to the temptation and ends up seduced by her sweets. In the film the patriarchal oppression of the Church is overcome by the restoration of the female spiritual power that has been refused by the Church.

The Da Vinci Code

The Da Vinci Code by Dan Brown, has also become an international best seller. A thriller novel much in the style of the film *Indiana Jones and the Last Crusade*, it too suggests the Church has been part of a huge conspiracy to cover up what really happened to Jesus: he got married to Mary Magdalene, had children and lived happily ever after. According to the myth promulgated by this book and other recent 'theories' about Jesus, the proper balance between male and female elements in Christianity and the presence of sexuality, were removed by the Church for the purpose of keeping and wielding power. The grail legend keeps this hidden Christian message alive and has to be recovered as patriarchal and oppressive Christianity is overthrown.

These kinds of fictions sometimes raise issues in the media about the indictment of the Church and Christians end up being first of all tarred with the same negative brush and then put in the position of having to defend the Church against accusers and detractors. But this is an invitation to close our own imaginations rather than explore with others. For example, *Chocolat* is an interesting novel, precisely because it has much to say about the power of listening, about appropriate and gentle pastoral care, about the importance of giving, and, in the recovery of Josephine, liberation of the oppressed and abused into their true identity. Instead of fighting for the Church *as it is portrayed in the novel*, we could simply enter imaginatively into the world of the chocolatier

and say what it teaches us about love and neighbour. We do not have to 'buy into' her Pagan beliefs or practice to do that, nor sell out our love of the gospel, but rather what the book tells us about being human.

His Dark Materials 🌐

In Philip Pullman's trilogy *His Dark Materials*, much has been made of his anti-Church stance. In these novels he represents 'God' (the 'Authority') and the 'Church'. These represent a kind of overarching parenthood whose overbearing regime reaches down into the world of the child and seeks to suppress imagination, exploration, change. The hound of heaven is not a sweet stalker but Fr Gomez, tracking the main character Lyra to prevent her from falling into sin and fulfilling the prophecy which will enable humans to be truly themselves at last. The overthrow of Metatron, the oppressive Regent and power who has held 'God' in thrall, allows liberation into a 'republic of heaven' in which no power, lordship or sovereignty holds sway. Yet this egalitarian vision is constantly suppressed by the Magisterium and by the theologians who do not want the children to pursue their own story and who will disable or kill them to make sure they present no threat.

Yet throughout Pullman's works are themes which resonate strongly and make sense within our own spiritual journey.[12] The creation is amazing, beautiful and diverse and Lyra and her friend Will are able to go from universe to universe discovering ever more extraordinary and amazing characters and animals. There is a creative energy within the universe which blows where it wills and that cosmic 'dust' must be allowed to flow freely or the world will stagnate and disappear. The worlds are themselves marked by betrayal and sacrifice and include not only the wonderful daemons as diverse and changing aspects of the children's selves or even souls, but also a liberation of the dead into an expansive reality of indwelling the creation. These kinds of themes mean something to Christians, but if we spend all our time apologising for 'criticism' and defending the indefensible manifestations of 'Church' in the novels, we cannot engage our imaginations and explore the spiritual journey laid out in the material properly.

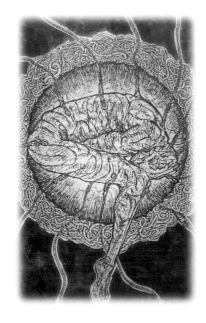

The Archbishop of Canterbury's dialogues with Philip Pullman have illustrated what it means to have generous and courteous discourse within the double spiral of spiritual engagement, providing a model we all could well follow in our own encounters with spiritual seekers

Science Fiction

The popularity of science fiction and science fantasy novels and films allow the creative imagination 'to boldly go where no man has gone before'. SF allows the exploration of all kinds of spiritual and metaphysical themes as we see in *Star Trek*, *Star Wars*, the *X files* ('the truth is out there') and other forms of the genre. In fiction, there can be very complex investigations of spiritual themes, from the wealth of the *Dune* material to the 'Culture' novels of Iain M Banks. To take just one example, in his Culture novel *Look to Windward*, Banks explores the nature of love and bereavement, guilt and revenge. In a universe in which heaven is not in doubt, a creature is sent to save those who cannot be admitted to heaven by sacrificing himself in an eye-for-an-eye act of revenge. His target is a godlike 'Mind' which cares for the lives of billions of sentient beings. The Mind takes pity on the creature sent to destroy it whose heart has been wrecked by the loss of his mate. It suffers with him and chooses to die with him, having taking upon itself the pain and the pity of the mad human urge to destroy others for power. It saves everyone – but it

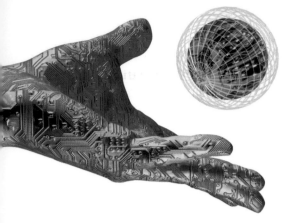

also exacts judgement on those who have used the creature's suffering to manipulate and betray him. In another of Banks' great science fiction explorations: *Excession*, a sign is sent from heaven, but technologically supreme humans and their sentient computers are so obsessed with conspiracy theories that they fail to perceive what it is. Against this story is set another narrative of infidelity and betrayal which has to be redeemed and restored. There is a moral lesson in that particular story for us all.

Abuse of imagination

Rescue us from the tyranny of our thoughts

In Alain Robbe-Grillet's novel *La Jalousie* (1957) the story is told through the imagination of a person who suspects his wife is having an affair. This doubt and suspicion corrupts everything he sees and creates a sense of intense mental strain. As readers of such a story, we are drawn into a world which is undermined by paralysing and destructive emotion. The imagination becomes twisted and corrupted until we cannot understand the 'truth' any more.

Many of us may be able to sympathise with such a viewpoint, but we may not realise just how badly negative thoughts and emotions like jealousy, covetousness and pride can twist and corrupt our imaginations so that we mis-read situations and colour them with our fantasies. Once doubt and mistrust take hold in our minds, we may not be able to cope with situations adequately and so our imaginative wondering and dreaming becomes full of fears, anxieties and mental suffering which we then project on to others. The Christian mystic Walter Hilton, in his book *The Ladder (Scale) of Perfection*, puts it like this:

All these stirrings will always boil out of thy heart, as water runneth out of the spring of a stinking well, and do hinder the sight of thy soul, that thou mayest never see nor feel clearly the love of Jesus Christ

Shakespeare examined the destructive power of jealousy within the human imagination in his play *Othello*, in which Othello, fed false information by Iago, begins to imagine his wife must be sleeping with another man. Suddenly every little word and action seems to prop up the distrust in his tormented imagination and, as jealousy takes hold, sense and reason depart from him and he descends into a hell of raving and horror in which his wife Desdemona must die.

The spiritual journey requires learning the ability to trust, to form open and honest relationships, to disclose our secrets, forgive our enemies and to give up our negative emotions. Within the Church, the act of confession and repentance has allowed Christians to examine the abuse of the imagination which can so quickly take hold in us and to let it go. But for many people inside and outside the Church, this process is seen as restrictive and guilt inducing, rather than equipping us with a language of liberation, freedom and new beginning. Our spiritual journey requires us to learn this language as a means of growing closer to God. Nor is this a spiritual discipline to be taken lightly – giving up fear, hatred, mistrust and guilt can be exceptionally hard, because these feelings actually feed our imagination and nurture it. When they are gone, we may feel peace but also emptiness. What are the *good* feelings and emotions which expand our imagination?

Negative emotions

Think of a time when you felt intensely jealous, covetous, angry, guilty or mistrustful. Imagine telling the story of how you felt to another person, setting the scene or background and explaining your role within it.

❖ **What details might you exaggerate, change or leave out altogether?**

❖ **What did that experience of negative emotion do to you and how have you/might you overcome it?**

❖ **What did the experience teach you?**

The spirals entwined, imagining with others

Films

Going to the cinema, buying or renting DVD films is an overwhelmingly popular activity in our western society.

Cinema attendance by age, 1984–2001: Social Trends 33
The proportion of adults attending the cinema has increased over recent years. Frequent cinema attendance in Great Britain has consistently been highest among those aged between 15 and 24. In 2001, 50 per cent of this age group reported attending the cinema once a month or more compared with 15 per cent of those aged 35 and over. The success of 'family' films such as *Shrek* and *Cats and Dogs*, with the third and fifth highest takings in the UK box office in 2001, may have contributed to recent increases in attendance among those aged between 7 and 14. The type of films released through mainstream cinemas tend to be large budget blockbusters and the increase in cinema attendance may be related to the expansion and investment in multiplex cinemas across the country. In addition to the multiplexes, smaller independent cinemas cater for more specialist 'art house' audiences.[6]

Engaging with people about films may be one of the most effective ways of exploring imaginatively with each another about where we are in our spiritual journey.

Films such as *The Lord of the Rings* trilogy and *The Matrix* trilogy have generated huge amounts of discussion and debate about the themes within the films and if we do not become imaginatively involved in such debate, the discussions will simply go on without Christian input. Yet we have so much to contribute to films which emerge from an unarticulated Christian background and which deal with fundamental issues of theology.

But perhaps we should give people the chance to explore films other than those in which we might be seen to have a sense of ownership or vested interest. Why shouldn't people going to see *Donnie Darko* or M Night Shyamalan's films be offered the chance to explore their experience of the film with us?

Watch a film

Revisit your favourite film (it doesn't have to be a 'deep' or 'spiritual' choice).

❖ **Why do you enjoy this film so much?**
❖ **Why is it important to you?**
❖ **How does the film engage your imagination or emotions?**
❖ **What would you say if you were to recommend the film to a friend?**

Now imagine doing this activity in terms of your Christian life.

Imagining: journeying into Christian tradition

The opening door

In C S Lewis' story *The Lion, the Witch and the Wardrobe*, the wardrobe famously opens into another world, a world in which the children in the story confront the forces of good and evil. We are called by God to open doors for people to glimpse another world, another way of life, another way of being, not to insist that they follow this path or that path within that world, but to explore it, wander where they will and come back to us full of questions and ideas about their experiences. They will have met Aslan, but it may be up to us to help them discover who he is.

So we have to be careful to make sure that people can get into the wardrobe in the first place and get a glimpse of that other world which is the world of our own spiritual journey. People cannot walk our spiral path of exploration if we keep putting obstacles in their way. What then can we do to provide such tantalising glimpses of our Christian life and to offer invitations to walk in our world?

Reimagine your church

The poet George Herbert wrote poetry when he let his imagination be inspired by every part of the church where he was vicar. He was inspired by the shapes he found in his church – his poem *The Altar* is laid out in an altar shape, but also by thinking about and meditating on the experience of being in his church for the sacraments and festivals. In effect, he entered into the world provided by the church building and explored every part of it in prayer, poetry and praise. Today we have even more possibilities:

Church of Fools is an attempt to create holy ground on the net, where visitors can worship, pray and talk about faith. The church is intended for people on the edges (and beyond) of faith, and for Christians from all church traditions.[7]

When this 'virtual church' was set up on the internet, it was flooded with people coming to visit it. Only a few such people could enter as complete characters within the church, but other visitors could enter as 'ghosts' and wander round the building investigating its world and praying or praising as they felt the need. For some people, the attraction seemed to be that the virtual church was rather like a computer game in which a new environment is explored and opens up to new worlds once you have completed a level and got to know it thoroughly.

How could we see our own churches imaginatively in order to provide people with hints of the world we would like them to explore? Once people enter our worlds, what do we have to engage their imagination and spiritual response? What else could we do to suggest that we want them to go further and experience the world of our worship, our community, our hospitality, our vision of kingdom?

Working together imaginatively 🌐

Silvia Dimitrova asked Canon Graham Kings to record on tape a passage in John 20. She prayed, listened and painted. This is the result:

In response, Graham wrote this poem:

Rabbouni

Who is this woman facing this man?
Head lightly inclined,
eyes wide open, gazing;
Hands uplifted, palms upward, surprised;
Gorgeously arrayed.

Who is this man facing this woman?
Coming from the right,
Profile clear, bearded,
Hand outstretched, palm down,
Gloriously appareled.

Behind her, two angels hover
Reflecting her shape:
Behind him, scented trees lean
setting the scene:
Below her, a dark opening hints.
All silent witnesses.
The eyes have it:
focus of tension and attention.
One word awakes her: 'Mary.'
One word responds: 'Rabbouni.'

Their hands shape a triangle
At the centre of meeting:
Her two, shocked and suppliant,
His one, blessing, calming, sending.

Graham Kings, 11 September 2004, on a painting by Silvia Dimitrova 'Rabbouni'

? **How could you form partnerships with others to explore the Christian faith in imaginative ways**

Visit your church

How much is there to explore within your church world?

What could be done to enhance the exploratory experience in your place of worship through the imagination?

Labyrinth ⊕

One of the most imaginative projects for spiritual exploration in recent times has been the installation of labyrinths in different churches. The purpose of the labyrinth is to set out a prayer walk or pilgrimage within a small space.[8] People are encouraged to walk the winding route into the heart of the labyrinth, perhaps stopping at waystations for special moments of prayer and meditation. At the centre of the labyrinth is usually some marker or other reminder of God. Here, walkers are invited to pause, rest and reflect, before journeying outward again to rejoin the world. In this respect, the labyrinth is another version of the double spiral. When we walk this path, we are not all going in the same direction, but when we find people going in a different direction, then we have the chance of encounter. When we pause in our journey towards the centre, the spiritual heart, we may find others alongside us who have come in by another route.

In one church in New Zealand, a labyrinth was constructed outside to act as a place for repentance and healing. As people began their journey they were first confronted by an installation of human wreckage including scrapped cars. At the second station, they were invited to contemplate a cross covered in empty wine bottles and running with water, and finally they were faced with a huge volcanic rock blazing with flame. These intense images had a profound effect on people both inside and outside the church. One visitor found in the flaming rock an extraordinary vision of an almighty God.

Think about the labyrinth

What was the New Zealand labyrinth trying to say to people through its stations?

. . . .

Where have we been?

This chapter has asked us to consider the role of the imagination in the task of exploring our own spirituality and sharing our faith with others.

❖ Imagination allows us to open up our mental worlds and to use our memories and experience to wonder and dream. Our imagination needs to be stimulated and fed in order to engage in creative exploration. Within our imagination, God can engage with us, provoke us, empower us, and challenge us.

❖ Scripture tells us about the role of dreams and vision in biblical times and dreams are still important to people today. Many people have powerful spiritual experiences which they treasure but may not repeat to anyone, least of all a Christian friend or minister. It takes special listening skills to access what has happened in their imagination.

❖ We can also engage with the imagination of God by meditating on the extraordinary nature of creation and by broadening our exploration of knowledge and ideas, come to know more of the breadth of God's mighty works.

❖ People with mental illness often experience a breakdown of the imaginative function, leaving them frightened and confused. Jesus gives us models of healing for those who endure this kind of hurt and it is our task to walk alongside our friends and neighbours in distress and to receive whatever they can tell us or show us of their spiritual lives.

❖ Different kinds of popular fiction offer us models of imaginative exploration, but we can become bogged down with 'criticisms' of Church. Rather, through engagement with such writing, we can build platforms of imaginative interaction between ourselves and others and to find common spiritual threads and themes.

❖ The imagination can nonetheless become populated by negative emotions such as jealousy and hatred which distort spiritual exploration and drag us away from knowledge and love of God. Because all of us are subject to sin, we need to acknowledge ways of purging the imagination of such colouring and the need in all of us for restoration and healing.

❖ Films are an incredibly popular form of cultural entertainment. Through films, we can reach out to others and engage them in imaginative exploration of the stories we see on the screen.

❖ Through re-imagining our church to see its possibilities for wonder, awe and mystery, we can offer people a journey into a new world. But we must not stop there, because we want to offer even more worlds for exploration: worlds of worship, fellowship and community. How can we make those worlds even more attractive to the spiritual seeker?

Prayer

Lord, open the door
and call us through
into unimagined worlds....
Amen

The
Continuing
Journey

Why do theology like this?

Religion vs spirituality?

This book has to do with the mission of the Church in the world, our world. But why on earth should the Church bother with its mission, if the trend is towards not only decline of its traditions, but multiple expressions of spirituality outside the Church are spreading like wildfire through our communities? Surely the apologetic tradition has failed and the self-defined spirituality of the current generation is overrunning a Church whose options have run out? This book has sought to show that this is a false view. The phenomenon we observe has to do with the theological and spiritual languages available to people in our western society, which have diverged and grown apart. When we fail to speak each other's languages gaps and holes start to appear in the way we can offer, share and make sense of our experiences of faith. We can already see this divergence in our own Christian languages, if we care to look, in the way we have steadfastly ignored the fresh expressions of Christian understanding coming into the western tradition from the missionary experience of other cultures and peoples. So instead of celebrating when the Holy Spirit dances, we become spiritually deaf, blind and dumb to what God is doing in our world.

Yet God speaks *everyone's* language, so we should not be surprised when people respond to the work of the Holy Spirit outside the Church and signs of spiritual search and spiritual journey spring up everywhere around us. The Pentecost experience is one of joining in with God's own ability to flood people's minds and hearts with his presence: 'in our own languages we hear them speaking about God's deeds of power' (Acts 2:11). When the apostles receive the Holy Spirit they are given surprised and grateful insight into how God speaks into every person's situation. Our own task, then, the Christian story and our story, grows out of this Pentecostal understanding, but have we forgotten the God of surprises? The Church exists to speak and be spoken to by every community, in recognition and exploration of God's 'deeds of power'. If we seem to have forgotten this, then we need to re-learn it. Once again we have to be the people of Pentecost and not only repeat Peter's words, but understand their importance in our own society: 'For the promise is for you, for your children, and for all who are far away, everyone whom the Lord our God calls to him' (Acts 2:39).The Pentecost experience undoes the chaos and confusion of Babel, but not by imposing one common language; instead it gives us a picture of mutual intelligibility, deep understanding and mutuality within diversity. Pentecost does not annul Babel but God redeems with diversity. This, then, is our task: to journey with all kinds of different and diverse people, and speak God's language to them, the gracious speech that overcomes all barriers, and to receive that language back from them. Once again we must recover the prophetic witness of the early church, when Paul and the apostles stood among the manifestations of spiritual quest all around them.

Within the double spiral, we walk our own journey and meet those who worship at the altar of the unknown god. It is true that in doing

> Then Paul stood in front of the Areopagus and said, 'Athenians, I see how extremely religious you are in every way. For as I went through the city and looked carefully at the objects of your worship, I found among them an altar with the inscription, 'To an unknown god'. What therefore you worship as unknown, this I proclaim to you. The God who made the world and everything in it, he who is Lord of heaven and earth, does not live in shrines made by human hands, nor is he served by human hands, as though he needed anything, since he himself gives to all mortals life and breath and all things. From one ancestor he made all nations to inhabit the whole earth, and he allotted the times of their existence and the boundaries of the places where they would live, so that they would search for God and perhaps grope for him and find him – though indeed he is not far from each one of us. For in him we live and move and have our being... *Acts 17: 22–8*

so we also meet people who worship idols, but then that is just as true of some Christians. In this midst of this searching, in the blind alleys and the roads to Damascus, our faith requires us to make the connections which enable us to affirm the spiritual search in people and to enable them to encounter, recognise and name Christ for themselves. The double spiral should enable us to meet again and rejoice with Dionysius the Areopagite and Damaris, but also to continue to walk with those who scoff (Acts 17:32–4). In some ways there is not enough 'scoffing' at us; perhaps our greatest danger is that other spiritual wayfarers claim *already to know* what Christian life is about, and view with benign indifference what they see as a quaint and old-fashioned variety of vaguely spiritual searching. In a strange way we need to teach other wayfarers *to scoff better*. We need to be a model not of 'religious experiences' which everyone can smile at, but of sensual lives, transformed and deepened by God's healing touch, which challenge, inspire and disturb those who travel with us.

The double spiral does not mean that we encounter other spiritual languages uncritically. Our journey through the senses has told us that the facility of attention is especially important. As Christians, we enter into a pattern of discipleship, but that doesn't mean we have nothing else to learn. We have to learn a new kind of listening, so that our encounter with the spirituality of others may nourish and sustain, but also challenge and change us. That listening should also help us to identify damaged and damaging languages, which themselves need challenging or are in need of healing and repair. One of the special tasks of Christian evangelism is not to *force* people to speak our language, but to help them transform their own languages in ways that they themselves acknowledge they need. There are gaps, hesitations and silences where the spiritual journey has not provided enough of the grammar people need to feel they have found what they seek. As Christians we believe that God transforms not only words, but also changes silences into encounters with God. There is always more to say to God, about God, to each other, and that may mean more talk or it may mean more attentive silence. God's eternal Word in the person of Jesus, can literally 'make sense' of what people have been searching for, so that at last they can say it for themselves, say 'yes' to the God who eternally says 'yes' to them.

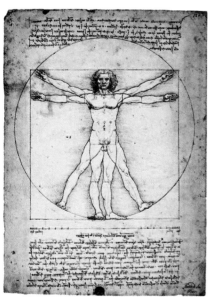

Vitruvian Man by Leonardo da Vinci.

Body languages

It is tempting to think of the language of the body as the first common language we have with every other human being; it seems so basic to being human. As human beings, we experience the world through our senses, so our sense-making takes place through a 'grammar' of body experience that coincides with that of others in a fundamental way. Yet we have seen how body languages are *languages*, with meanings, nuances and associations. Not all body language grammars are alike. What we have done is to try to show how these experiences connect with people searching for faith outside the church and how those connections form bridges through which new languages of mutual learning may themselves be learned. Ours is a sense-making faith.

When Irenaeus says that 'the glory of God is a living man', he is making a Christological statement. When we explore our body languages we do this not only in awe and gratitude towards the Creator, but also because our sensate male and female bodies can become living memories of Christ's own body, that was born, experienced our life, was crucified, died, was buried and rose again from the dead. In this sense, our particular Christian body languages show themselves as a fascinating bodily dialect. Our task is to show what *difference* that makes within the double spiral of spiritual journeying. Our own exploration of these body languages, these 'grammars' of sense experience should not simply melt into the pool of shared experience, even 'religious' experience, because our own sense-making, which propels us in our own journey, takes place within the knowledge of the Easter experience. Walter Brueggeman argues that Jesus' resurrection is the 'ultimate energising of a new future'. It is that energy that informs the way we learn our body languages and transforms them. We are not just spiritual people investigating the wonder of nature; our particular spiritual experience as Christians is transformative. The grace of God permeates our world in ways which affect our spiritual perceptions and reactions. So we understand in mission that the Christian commitment, sustained by Word and sacraments, must result in real change within the world. Our journey is not aimless, but directed towards God's purposes.

So we can move from the contemplation of Jesus as God's son incarnate in a real physical body to the understanding of the Church as the Body of Christ. St Paul indicates that Jesus's physical human body was limited to a particular period of time and space, but that his Body continues to exist in community. Moreover, every aspect of Jesus's ministry is part of that Body and must work to transform the world to become as God intends. Our body languages are the medium through which we make it known that the Body of Christ is not an abstract concept, but an organic witness to the work of God in the world. The Church in its final and best form, in all its range and diversity, is the Body at work, glorifying God by being alive and by using its sense-making faith to change brokenness into beauty.

The theology of the physical body and of the Body of Christ is important because of its relation to the brokenness and fragmentation we see around us. We have had to acknowledge the shadow side, the fact that we live in a broken world contaminated by human disobedience

and sin. In the journey chapters we have reminded ourselves that we can abuse our bodies and use our bodies to abuse others in so many different ways. Many people outside the Church are aware of the presence of evil or brokenness in the world around them – and their spirituality struggles to take account of it – yet their perception of the Church is that it is obsessed by a negative, condemnatory language of sin. Our exploration of our body languages should enable us to share the understanding that through Christ we have access to redemption, reconciliation and transformation of that brokenness into healing. These are the 'grammars' which people more readily understand and which we must now explore with them, replacing the language which has been misunderstood with that of love.

Journeying together

Our spiritual journey, as it spirals out into the world around us, carries the stamp of Christ's uniqueness and distinctiveness. We are Christ's people, Christians, and that marks and shapes how we grow as spiritual people. But that distinctiveness is more than a set of identifiers; living in Christ means that we cannot help but be infected by the mission of God in Christ. What is recognisable about us is that we live and grow in this particular life. At the same time, how does this journey allow us to find out what 'bad grammars' we have in our Christian discourse, to free ourselves from a language that prevents us from sharing honestly and openly with others and which then permits us to speak the language of love?

The double spiral, where could we find ourselves?

Another important function of doing theology in this way is to give permission for missionary apologetic to be set within the context of wonder, exploration, play, dreaming and imagination. Too often, the way we are nurtured, taught, trained within the Christian faith, locks us into a model of faithfulness that brooks no experiment, no looking outside the box, no flirting with anything difficult, baffling or dangerous, and quite possibly no fun.

In the *Godly Play* sessions, the heart of the experience is when the precious gold box is opened to reveal the elements for journeying into a story of God. Those elements are the same for each telling of that particular story, but how the story is told depends on the ability of those present to be seized with wonder at what would or could happen next. We hope this book and the accompanying website is the start of just such a way of sharing faith and involving others in that experience of wonder, gratitude and delight. And our journey, indeed our whole Christian life, is participation in a never-ending story of God's gracious deeds. This language of love is one of endless possibility....

Finding ourselves in worship

'Sense making faith' implies more than a set of intellectual arguments or even equipping ourselves with a 'grammar' of spiritual insight and understanding. All Christian activity, searching and exploration finds its way inevitably into worship. But we will not 'end up' in worship, but find that worship is the means to open up and to pass through, equipped for God's mission and our work in the world, led by the Spirit. What we offer to God in worship is our souls and bodies, and this worship equips our physical human lives as means of witness and transformation in the culture around us.

In the experience of Eucharist, all the aspects of our sense making faith come together, as we have described through the chapters. The Eucharist holds the spirals of our spiritual journeys together and reaches out to touch and heal the journeys of those who are still seeking. The Eucharist provides powerful images of brokenness: bread that is broken, wine that is poured out and turns these into images of healing, for the bread and wine is Jesus: 'only say the word and I shall be healed'. The Eucharist reaches out to all our senses and requires us to make the words of Jesus among his friends at the Last Supper, words of affirmation and assent which resonate far beyond the confines of Church: This is my Body.

Exploring the Journey Points Together

Note to group leaders

This section contains material for use by group leaders and is for using *Sense Making Faith* in a group setting. The first part is an introductory session, but after this the group material has a common format as follows:

Starting out – Groups can first be encouraged to look at what gifts and resources you have already relating to the physical sense discussed in each chapter and to think about how those assets can be developed.

Going deeper – An activity related to broadening out the exploration of the sense in question.

Entering the world of – An activity related to the absence of the particular sense.

Reaching out – An activity which seeks to engage people outside the church through the sense in some way.

Celebrating – An activity to build up fellowship and confidence within your group – which may involve doing something outside the session environment out in the community.

Praying together – Each session ends with ideas for prayer and reflection.

You can mix and match these suggested activities depending on the time and space available and the interests and makeup of your particular group. Alternatively, you can do the various activities sequentially over a number of shorter sessions.

Plain text versions of the group material are available on the website for download or alternatively by email, on disk or as a powerpoint presentation from anne.richards@c-of-e.org.uk.

Introduction to the Journey

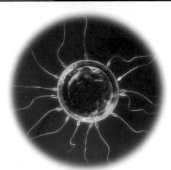

Purpose of the journey

To introduce the theme of journey by physical movement around a space.

To open up awareness of the world, ourselves and our senses.

To equip people to meet others on their spiritual journeys.

The activities in this particular session are designed to form an introduction to the rest of the material in *Sense Making Faith* so it is quite a long process if done in one session and will take up to a whole day. With any group, try to use the space (even a small space) in such a way that people move from point to point, from a beginning point to an end point. In a large space, this might mean moving from a wall or floor with displayed pictures, to different open areas with chairs. If there is limited space, ask people to move to a different chair at each journey point, so that they have a slightly different view and situation at each one. At each transition, people will need a short space to settle and become ready for the next activity or experience. Separate activities are indicated with a symbol.

Depending on the type of group and the time and space available, you can add or omit sections, or you can run this introductory material in a series of short sessions using link modes, such as a picture or prayer carried over to the next session as a reminder.

There are five sections to this introductory material including: working with pictures together with discussion; meditation with optional video; games and imagining; bible study; prayer.

1. Activity: Wonders of the world
Preparation

Collect photos of some 'wonders' of the world, including any local 'wonders' – anything that catches the attention. You can look at the website www.spiritualjourneys.org.uk for ideas and downloadable

pictures. ⊕ *Spread the photos out on a table or floor or mount them on a board so people can look at different ones.*

There are four elements to this activity: choosing photos, discussing the photos, discussing practical issues about your church, prayer and thanksgiving. You can mix and match these as appropriate.

● Ask people to choose a photograph that means something to them. Allow people to look at each other's choices and compare them.

● Discuss in the group:

   For photos and images which show natural wonders
   ○ What about this catches the attention?

   ○ Why would you want to photograph this or remember it?

   ○ How does looking at this 'wonder' make you feel?

   For photos and image which are manufactured wonders
   ○ What kind of person or persons made this?

   ○ What would it take to make it?

   ○ What skills or other qualities would you need to make it?

● Discuss and record:

   ○ In what ways do local church buildings catch people's attention?

   ○ What could *we* do to get people to stop and wonder about the local church?

   ○ What skills have people got in our own community for people to wonder at?

   ○ In what ways could local talents and skills be used to make things which would attract people's attention and interest?

● Conclude this session by thanking God for the wonder and beauty of creation and for the extraordinary variety of human skills. Pray that such skills be used to create beautiful and useful things and not used to hurt or destroy.

2. Meditation: Being Human

Preparation

Make a short (five minute) video recording of a sports programme, or arts programme such as dance. Or use short sections of an exercise video. The section of the film Billy Elliott *where he is bouncing on the bed, running or dancing, along with his description of how he feels when he is dancing might be helpful. If you are using this material in a day session, you could think about involving a children's dance or gymnastic team to demonstrate their skills.*

● Ask the group to move to a new location, then sit on chairs or on the floor.

● Watch the video or presentation if you are using this.

   Ask the group to remove their shoes (where practical), close their eyes, put their hands in their laps and sit quietly and comfortably until relaxed. Ask them to become aware of their bodies breathing, their hearts beating, their digestive system working, their sense of the temperature, their clothes against skin.

Encourage people to imagine looking inwards at their own bodies. Think about the amazing nature and intricacy of the internal workings of the human body. Are we aware that we are alive? Think about the precious gift of health and how we should not abuse our bodies or take its health for granted.

- Ask the group to think about the potential of the human body, its strength, endurance and athletic abilities. Why do we admire great athletes such as Kelly Holmes, Paula Radcliffe, Jonah Lomu, Steve Redgrave, Tanni Grey-Thompson, and the late Jane Tomlinson?

- Conclude by thanking God that we are fearfully and wonderfully made. Thank God for the example of those who show us human beings fully alive in their physical abilities and gifts.

3. Games, imaginings: Appreciating our senses
Preparation

Some excerpts from Terry Waite's Taken on Trust, *or Brian Keenan's* An Evil Cradling *might help set the mood. You will need pens and paper, ice cubes, apples and potatoes, scarves, etc, if you want to play the various games mentioned below. You will need a scented candle, a bowl of cut oranges or lemons and a tape or CD player with appropriate music if you want to do the meditation.*

- Ask the group to move to a new location, and put chairs in circle.

- Ask the group for any brief stories of temporary sensory deprivation, such as injury or operation. Ask story tellers to explain what it was like to be deprived of the senses. What was it like to recover?

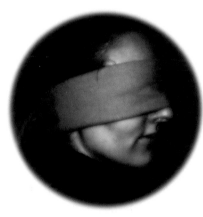

- Imagine together and discuss the experience of being held hostage in solitary confinement for several years, as Terry Waite was, for example. Ask the group to imagine:

  ○ Being blindfolded all the time;

  ○ Being blasted with radio white noise so you can't hear coherent sounds or experience silence;

  ○ Being given nothing to eat but stale bread;

  ○ Being forced to remain in a room smelling of excrement and vomit;

  ○ Being unable to move until you can't feel the sense of touch.

  🗨 **Ask the group what things might sustain them if they were in this sort of situation.**

- You can play sensory deprivation games together such as:

  ○ Blind man's buff/pin the tail on the donkey/draw a pig blindfold and sign it;

  ○ Chinese whispers;

  ○ Hot or cold (put an ice cube on a blindfolded person's arm);

  ○ Apple or potato (ask a blindfolded person holding their nose to tell which);

  ○ Ask the children in your local school, church or fellowships for variations of these games and ask them to teach your group how to play them.

💬 **Discuss: how did playing the games make people in the group feel?**

● Prayer and meditation

Light a scented candle and perhaps play some meditative music or lay out a bowl of oranges or cut lemons. Conclude by thanking God for our senses and sense experiences. Bring before God all those whose humanity is being denied by being hostages or unlawfully imprisoned. Are there those in your own community whose ability to be fully alive is being compromised? What could be done about it?

4. Bible Study

Preparation

Give each member of the group a copy of the Bible passage John 12:1–8. You can photocopy the passage from the text in this book, or download it from the website. 🌐 *Or people can use their own bibles.*

● Relocate the group and assemble in a seated group suitable for bible study and prayer together.

● Ask a suitable group member to read John 12:1–8. This passage can also be used as a role play.

● Questions:

  ○ What is Judas really complaining about and how do we know he has become an 'outsider'?

  ○ How does this passage compare with the accounts of the Last Supper?

  ○ What is the importance of the body and the physical senses in the passage?

  ○ How does this passage help us to think about worshipping the Lord?

5. Prayer

Preparation

Make copies of St Teresa's prayer for group members, or write it up on a board for people to look at. You can photocopy the prayer from the introduction or download it from the website. You can include an image or icon for focus, or a candle.

● Move to a final location around an image, or in a circle.

  ○ *Say together*

    Lord,
    We offer you our souls and bodies
    Use our bodies to bear witness to your truth
    Help us to walk the journey
    Searching for signs of you
    Delighting in finding you
    Making friends
    Being disciples
    Amen

Journey Points for Seeing

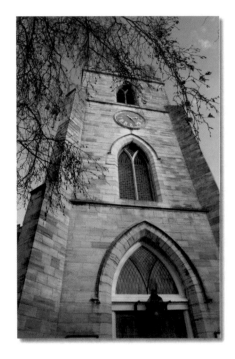

Purpose of the journey

To learn to use our eyes for God.

To learn more about the spiritual journeys of those around us.

To help others discover more about God through visual resources.

1. Starting out. What have we got?
Preparation

It is possible to start this session by going into your place of worship and asking people to take a good look at whatever they can see.

This section has five questions for discussion by the group, but you can use just one or two of them if you prefer, or as time allows.

- Ask the group to think about how people outside or on the fringes of the Church might encounter Jesus through your own local church situation.

- What will non churchgoers see in our place of worship when it is empty?

  In discussion of the question it can help to make a list of items in response to these supplementary questions:

  ○ What parts of our place of worship explain our faith visually?

  ○ How can people find out what different things are for and why they matter?

  ○ What else could we have in our place of worship visually to teach people about the basics of Christian faith?

- Ask the group to consider the question:

  🐾 **How do people learn what goes on in the Church if visitors come when it is empty?**

  Lead the group in a discussion of what resources you have to show people visually what goes on in your place of worship. Do you have photographs of people in your building? Do you have videos or DVDs available for enquirers to show them what happens at a wedding or baptism? If you have any visual resources of this kind, you could review them with the group and consider whether they are up to date and capable of generating attention.

  Make a list of any visual resources you have to offer visitors and make a decision to add at least one more. This could then be a practical outcome by the group, to put up photographs showing what happens in your place of worship or make a short video.

- Ask the group to consider the question:

  🐾 **What visual signs are there that the congregation, no matter how few, actually loves and cares for your place of worship and for the Christian faith?**

  Discuss and make a list with the group about the things which go on 'behind the scenes' such as cleaning, doing the flowers, polishing the silver, washing linen, running off service sheets or making kneelers.

Discuss the proposition that if one of the most important evangelistic resources is communicating the idea that we love our place of worship and want to honour and praise God through caring for it, how will a person coming into our building know that the people who come here love it?

● Ask the group to consider if there are any areas in which the church could be better loved and cared for and if so what resources you have to do so.

2. Going deeper: seeing the familiar differently
Preparation

Find an unusual image of the crucifixion or other religious scene, which can be mounted for display or otherwise shown to the group. If you are unable to find a suitable image, look at the downloadable material on the website. ⊕ *You might want to use fairy lights or indoor sparklers for part of the session.*

● Spend some time in a group looking at the image and then share together what you think and feel about it.

● Other activities in which the group can explore the familiar differently include:

○ Ask the group to get into pairs and to look into each other's faces. Ask each of the pair in turn to describe to the other what they see.

○ Ask members of the group who wear glasses to take them off and look at some illuminated fairy lights or an indoor sparkler. Ask them to describe what they see. Ask the group to consider what is different about their experience to normally sighted individuals?

3. Entering the world of the blind

● Work together in the group to re-write a bible story from the point of a blind person, eg the birth of Jesus, the haul of fish, the crucifixion or the resurrection appearances. There are also examples already done on the website which you can use if you prefer. ⊕

4. Reaching out to others: advent calendars

(This is a Christmas activity, but if you want to do this activity at another time of year, you can still adapt the activity to fit the season.)

Preparation

Ask group members, or find examples yourself of secular advent calendars, including any that have sweets or chocolate included. Try to find religious calendars to compare them with. You will also need craft materials, pictures, cards etc to make the alternative calendar.

● Ask the group to examine the calendars and discuss what messages are being sent by them. You can also eat the chocolate or sweets in the process!

Invite the group to design and make an advent calendar. Use pictures from the internet, pictures drawn by children or bits of Christmas cards and stick them on to a large piece of card with lift up flaps or contained in envelopes so that they tell the Christmas story. The images can be traditional or contemporary.

- The advent calendar you make as a group can be further used to imagine or role play the Christmas story. The advent calendar can also be used in schools or displayed on a notice board outside the church – perhaps one image per day.

- You can also organise the group to make other kinds of calendar or story board to fit with the liturgical year or to tell bible stories. Discuss with the group other ways inside and outside your church to encourage others to open the envelope or look behind the door to see what's inside or behind.

5. Celebrating being church together: a visual journey

Preparation

Decide on what kind of visual journey from the options below is most appropriate for your group and get the materials together.

- Options include:
  - Using the stations of the cross as a visual journey. If this is not a tradition in your place of worship and you want to explore the stations with the group, you can use online versions projected on to a screen, or downloaded from internet sites, such as http://www.ewtn.com/devotionals/stations/face.htm.
  - Use the images from *The Christ We Share* CMS third edition:
  - See Jesus through the eyes of Christian artists from Africa, Asia, and Latin America. This will enable the group to experience representations of Christ from around the world and explore understanding of Jesus; learn about different world theologies; and discover what this means for the community.

    Go to http://www.cms-uk.org for this resource.
  - Use the Stations of the Cross journey or the images of Jesus from our spiritual journeys website.

6. Praying together

Spend some time together in silent prayer and meditation perhaps around a candle or an image.

Lead the session to a close by using this prayer or any other appropriate prayer you prefer. Alternatively, you can photocopy the prayer from this page and say it together as a group.

> Lord,
> The world is a beautiful creation
> Brought into being by you
> Sustained by you
> Loved by you.

We have broken and hurt your world,
We have hurt its created life,
And left it in pain

Teach us to be agents of your healing power
To find you in the light
To find you in the darkness
To bring the hope of restoration

Amen

Journey Points for Hearing

Purpose of the Journey

To learn to use our ears for news of God.

To explore what other people are hearing.

To make connections between our spoken and musical traditions and theirs.

1. Starting out: what have we got?

Preparation

Bring some Christian music (hymns, organ music, carols etc) on a CD or a tape.

● Begin this item by asking the group to spend a few minutes together in silence. Ask the group to concentrate on all the noises around them, both externally and within their own bodies.

After this make a list of the sounds on a board or flip chart.

 Discuss in the group what the noises might be telling us about our world and our bodies. What might God be saying if we only paid enough attention through these noises?

● For the second part of this item invite the group to listen to some familiar Christian music on a CD or a tape. You can then use the following questions to help the group explore the music tradition in your place of worship and its relevance to people who don't go to church.

○ What different kinds of music do we have in our worship? Is our music and singing something which engages everybody or is it there as a filler while something else (eg the collection) happens?

○ Who is involved in our music? (Is the music something which is left to a choir or music group, or is everyone encouraged to be part of the musical tradition of the church?) Who else could get involved in the music who isn't now?

○ What will visitors hear if they visit our place of worship? (For example: if your building is open to visitors do you have any taped worship music playing?) Is the music appropriate to visitors' needs (eg will there be times of silence?)?

As a result of this discussion, make a plan with the group to do one thing to improve any visitor's experience of what they hear.

2. Going deeper: what do hymns and worship songs mean?

Preparation

Make a CD or a tape of some well known hymns, anthems, carols or other worship songs. Have some hymn books available.

- Ask the group to look at the words of *Hark the Herald Angels Sing* (you can choose another commonly used hymn or carol if you prefer)

  Remind the group that Christmas, for example, is a time when we can expect to see people who only come on that one occasion. They will probably be familiar with at least some of the traditional carols.

  Work through the words of the carol with the group, and see if people could explain what it is about in simple language to a person who has never had anything to do with the Christian faith. One way to do this is to divide people into pairs or small groups and each work on a particular phrase, for example:

  - ❍ 'God and sinners reconciled';
  - ❍ 'Christ the everlasting lord';
  - ❍ 'late in time behold him come';
  - ❍ 'veiled in flesh the Godhead see';
  - ❍ 'the incarnate deity';
  - ❍ 'our Emmanuel'.

  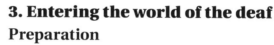 Conclude this section by asking the group to reflect together on how easy or difficult this task was.

3. Entering the world of the deaf

Preparation

Check the rules and process for the game Charades and prepare in advance some hymn titles or bible stories that lend themselves to mime. If doing the last activity, make a short video of a section of any popular TV programme/advertisement or use a video or DVD film.

- Divide the group into teams. Explain the rules of Charades and ask the group to act out a hymn title or well known bible story for the others to guess. At the conclusion of this activity, ask people how hard they had to concentrate in order to understand what might be going on.

  Another way of doing this would be to choose a well known bible story such as the 'prodigal son' or 'the man fallen among thieves' and ask a few people to take on a role play only using mime. At the conclusion of the activity, ask the group whether it was difficult to work out what was happening without any words.

- Play a short excerpt of a TV programme or advertisement or film to members of the group, with the sound off. Ask the group to discuss afterwards what the characters were saying and what was going on. If you like, you can replay the excerpt and ask people to invent the dialogue in any creative way you like as it goes along.

  Conclude this section by asking the group to reflect on the experience – were there any aspects of the story which came out more strongly

because the story could not be 'told' in a straightforward way? How might being 'deaf' sharpen the attention to other things which are going on?

4. Reaching out to others: connecting with what others hear

Preparation

Ask some young people in your congregation, worship group or community to suggest some contemporary music for you to listen to. (If you already have young people in your group then perhaps they could lead this section in particular, or even the whole process.) Collect several kinds of music from different genres for playing to the group and if possible record some tracks from music videos.

Ask your worship leader, choir/organ master or other music leader about the most requested music at baptisms, weddings and funerals. You can also make a tape of some of these.

Relient K, a popular American 'Christian Rock' band.

● Play the music and video extracts to the group. Divide people into pairs and ask them to discuss:

○ Did you enjoy listening to the music? (Be honest!)

○ Was there any music that connected to your own spiritual journey? If so, in what way?

○ Were there things about the music that you found difficult to hear or to understand?

 **Round this off by collecting the positive and negative feedback from the whole group.**

● If possible, invite young people in your congregation or community to come to the session to share their own feelings about their favourite music and what it means to them. If you have people in your congregation or fellowship who go clubbing, ask them to describe the attraction of the music and the clubbing community.

● Discuss with the group the kinds of music used for the occasional offices in your church. What kinds of music or hymns are most popular? Have you come across any unusual requests? Does your church or fellowship have a standard set of music possibilities for these occasions? What could be done to engage people's own spiritual journeys more effectively?

 Ask the group for suggestions for one thing that could be done in your situation to engage more effectively through music those people who don't often come to church.

5. Celebrating being church together

Preparation

Work with others such as a local school, or your church choir to organise an activity such as a concert, carol singing, Songs of Praise evening or other music making activity and try to involve the local community.

● Involve the group in your musical evening and gather together for feedback.

- If a musical event is impossible, or you want to keep to the group session, watch the excerpt from the film *Sister Act* where the singing of Salve Regina brings young people in off the street. Another film excerpt might be the scene in *The Blues Brothers* where Jake sees the light in James Brown's church. Make sure these films are suitable for your group's ages. Ask the group what the excerpt suggests to them and discuss what kind of music would tempt people in from off the street in *your* area.

6. Praying together
Preparation

If you don't want to sing together, you will need a music tape or CD of suitable music.

- Spend some time together in prayer using a Taizé chant or listening to other meditative music such as Gregorian chant. Use the time to reflect on what God is saying through the music.

  Agree on a favourite hymn with the members of the group and hum it quietly together without articulating any of the words. Ask the group to pray the words through in their minds.

  Finish the time together with a period of complete silence.

Journey Points for Smell

Purpose of the journey

To become aware of the importance of smell in our lives.

To use awareness of smell to illuminate scripture and the way we worship.

To see shared smell experiences as a means of witness and learning from others.

1. Starting out: what have we got?
Preparation

Be prepared to take your group around your church or place of worship.

- Ask members of the group to walk around your place of worship and identify the prevailing smell. Ask them to consider what the smell is like? How welcoming is it?

  Ask the group to discuss in pairs what kinds of smell make people feel welcome, relaxed, open, receptive, happy, peaceful. In pairs, or small groups, think about what smells could be associated with praise, prayer, confession, etc.

2. Going deeper: identifying smells
Preparation

Ask members of your group to bring along examples of scents or scented products which they use frequently on their person or in their homes. For the last activity you will need to collect examples of different smells eg hay, lavender, camphor, disinfectant, coffee, a pine branch, etc.

- Using a flipchart or board, ask the group members to list all the smells about their person: soap, shampoo, cologne, deodorant, washing powder, foot spray, liniment etc. List these in two columns, one for men and one for women. How many different fragrances for men and women are present? Are there groups of scents common to the group?

- How good is your nose? Ask members of the group to bring along an example of a scented product they use frequently. Put these, unidentified, on a table and ask people to pick one not their own. Divide the group into pairs and get the pairs to try out their chosen scents and to try to identify who they belong to.

- Ask the group to think about the familiar scent of people they love and to describe how they would recognise them if they had to by smell alone.

- Provide examples of different distinctive smells. Ask members of the group to consider in pairs 'where were you when you last smelled this'?

- Encourage the unfolding of stories by permitting people to have continued access to the smell.

  🗨 **Discuss together: can shared smell bind us together as a loving community?**

3. Entering the stench

- Ask members of the group to list on a flipchart or board things that smell really bad. What do we think and feel about people who have to live with such smells? Where are the bad smells in the local community?

- Ask the group to consider what initiatives could the church be involved in, or is already involved in, to transform the 'bad' smells of the local community?

- Try to get the group to agree to engage in *one* thing which would help to transform the 'bad' smells within the community.

4. Reaching out to others
Preparation
With others, organise a wine or juice tasting to which people outside the church can be invited. Ask permission to use some of the wine you use for communion (unconsecrated) in the tasting session, which you can water down as appropriate.

- Organise a wine or juice tasting and ask people to concentrate on describing the smell of the drinks. The descriptions could be written on a board or on post it notes. Encourage people to be creative in their descriptions. The TV wine taster Jilly Goolden has even gone as far as to suggest she could smell 'wet dog' and 'rubber' in wine, so encourage people to be extravagant in their tasting descriptions. Make a note of what people say about the communion wine.

You can encourage the group to follow up any friendships made with others through this activity with an invitation card or a few lines about the Last Supper or Holy Communion.

5. Celebrating being Church together
Preparation

Collect examples of anything that will help imagine a bible story in terms of smell, eg cooked fish or meat, the hay of the nativity stable. There are examples on the website to help you. 🌐

- Take a familiar passage of scripture and study it together concentrating on the smell background and any imagery. Ask the group to consider if looking at scripture in this way brings out new perspectives and meanings. Ask the group to explore what being a disciple of Jesus would smell like.

6. Praying together
Preparation

Collect together items to create a perfumed environment for prayer: scented candles, incense, essential oils or other perfumes.

- Spend some time in silent meditation with perfume as a background. Ask people to concentrate on the scent and to imagine prayer being like a fragrance escaping from its source, permeating everything around with praise, petition or thanksgiving. Ask people to think how the scent can connect us with our memories, such that our whole lives can be offered to God and as a witness to his glory.

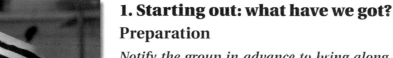

Journey Points for Touching

Purpose of the journey

To think about and understand how much of the world we encounter through touch.

To understand the importance of touch in creating community and relationship.

To understand the responsibility involved in touching others.

To use touch to heal and to reconcile.

1. Starting out: what have we got?
Preparation

Notify the group in advance to bring along their favourite fabrics or favourite pieces of clothing. If doing the second activity, you will need to ask people to bring along clothing contributions and bring or create a dressing-up box.

Dressing up

Use this especially to celebrate diversity within the group. Begin by encouraging people to bring their special fabrics or favourite item of clothing into a sacred space: this is my fabric. The items can be arranged or displayed if appropriate care is taken with them.

Ask the group to talk in pairs about why they chose their items. Or ask questions to draw out the stories the fabrics may bring with them, eg why is this sari silk important, why is this college scarf so full of memory? Allow people to touch the items with care and reverence and to experience what they feel like.

Role play

Make a dressing-up box and ask members of the group each to contribute an item – clothes, shoes, hats etc. Ask members of the group to find items in the dressing up box and to use the items in a role play. The role play can be an imaginary story or relate to a Bible story such as Joseph's coat, the nativity or the scene at the empty tomb.

Ask the group to discuss what would be found in the Church's dressing up box? Make a list of any items (eg altar cloths or vestments, banners etc) which might be found. What might people outside the Church make of such items? How could you explain to those people what such items are for?

2. Going deeper: experiencing touch
Preparation

Find someone in your community who is skilled at face painting and/or makeovers using cosmetics and ask them to be part of this activity. If you have children in your group, the children might enjoy the face-painting. Older people might prefer to be part of the make-over experience. Check that the volunteers' skin is suitable for the paint and cosmetics and check that the materials used are safe and non-allergenic. Make similar checks if using face masks, soap and flannels. You will also need towels and tissues, make-up remover etc for clean up afterward.

Face-painting

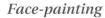

Introduce the face-painter(s) to the group. Ask the group to select a willing volunteer to have their face painted or to experience the makeover. Ask the face-painter to take the group through the process, explaining what is going on at each stage. Invite the group to comment and ask questions.

Ask the painter(s) what it was like to touch people's faces and change their appearance. Ask the painted people what the experience of being painted was like and how they feel about their new look.

Any men who feel this activity is not for them could be invited to try a face mask or simply have their face washed and dried carefully by another person.

Mask making

A very interesting, but more complex task is mask making. If you want to try this in your group you should first check out an excellent description of the technique and its implications for spiritual discovery in Olive M Fleming Drane's article *Making Masks, healing persons, and teaching Practical Theology* which is available on our website.

3. Entering the world of the untouchable
Preparation
Prepare a parcel of something like a small box of chocolates or bag of sweets as for a game of pass the parcel. You will a tape or CD player as you will need to control when the music stops and starts.

- Ask the group to sit in a widely spaced circle. Ask one person to volunteer to be an 'untouchable'. In a large group there could be several volunteers. Tell the group you are going to get them to play pass the parcel but that the untouchable is never allowed to receive or pass on the parcel or to touch anyone in the course of the game. You will need to control the music to make sure this happens. If the volunteer inadvertently gets hold of the parcel, stop the game and take it away from them.

When someone finally wins, you must direct that the chocolates or sweets are shared out among the group, except for the 'untouchable' volunteer who doesn't get anything.

💬 **Ask the group to discuss what it was like to exclude a member from the activity and ask the volunteer to share his or her experience of being left out. Share any memories of being excluded or shut out and what that feels like. Finish by re-including the member in the group by some appropriate act of touching and by sharing some other food or drink with them. Ask the volunteer to share any thoughts on what is it like to be 'back'.**

- Ask the question: who are the untouchables in our community? How could we reach out to them in Christian love? Ask the group to try to find *one* thing the local church could do to reach out to people who never get to join in.

4. Reaching out to others: touch-therapy, fabrics
Preparation

Invite someone from the local community or local hospital who practices some form of therapeutic touch therapy to come and talk about what they do and to give a talk or demonstration. It is advisable to invite somebody who only offers physical therapy for relief of symptoms (eg physiotherapy), not spiritual healing, which may cause confusion. The second activity requires prior planning for a community project involving fabrics. You could try to involve a sewing circle or knitting club, or anyone in your community who is good at craft and design. You will need fabric and frame materials for making the tent and sewing materials. You will need to give instructions about the project and commission the various parts of the construction.

- Introduce the person who is to talk about and demonstrate their touch-therapy. Members of the group can then be invited to ask questions, comment and to reflect on the talk or demonstration.

Tent-making

The artist Tracey Emin created a piece called *All the people I have ever slept with* in which she placed all the names of lovers and bedfellows in a tent. You could encourage the group to transform this idea by creating a 'tent of joy' using a large piece of fabric on a simple frame in which are placed or embroidered the names of people we love, or a 'tent of healing' for those who are sick and in need of Christ's healing, or a 'tent of remembrance' as a means of celebrating the lives of people who have died.

Ask the group to discuss this experience and then encourage them to draw up a list and send invitations to others outside the church to ask if they want to contribute a name to the tent or be involved in the project. You could also ask local schools if they want to be involved in such a project.

If it is not possible to make a tent, a large sheet can be hung on a wall and similarly decorated, preferably in a way that enables people to touch rather than just look.

4. Celebrating being church together: A Coat of many colours

Preparation

Following Peter Privett's inspiration from the chapter on touch, find an old liturgical garment or a large spare coat or robe. A long scarf or shawl would also do. Decide on a 'theme' for the coat, related to something current within the church. It could be a liturgical event of a theme such as 'reconciliation'. You will also need paper or card, safety pins, pens, pencils or paints.

Agree a suitable theme with the group. Bring the coat or scarf to the session and ask people to touch, hold and wear the garment while meditating on the chosen theme. Ask the group then to look for scripture texts and images relating to the theme and to write or paint the texts on to paper or card. These can be carefully pinned to the garment. Gradually build up layers of texts and images. When it is finished discuss with the group how to use the garment within the church's liturgy in whatever way is appropriate, whether as a sermon illustration, a prayer point or an interactive event.

● If you prefer, you could encourage the group to take the lead in another textile project such as a prayer quilt. There are lots of ideas for this at www.prayerquilt.org

5. Praying together

Preparation

If you have made a tent or hanging, this can be used for prayer. Otherwise bring to the session a selection of items with interesting textures (eg a stone, cotton wool, a feather, a flower, a pine cone etc) which people can choose to hold as they pray. Ask people to close their eyes and spend a few minutes exploring their item with their fingertips. Then lead the group in this, or another appropriate prayer.

Lord,
Your world comes to us
In softness and hardness
In the rough and the smooth.
We feel the warmth of your sunlight,
The cold sharpness of your frosty air.
Our faces know your drying wind
And the wet splash of spray and rain.
May our hands reach out to others

With healing and unbroken hope,
So that they may come to recognise
The perfect touch of your divine love.
Amen

Journey Points for Tasting

Purpose of the journey

To think about taste experiences.

To investigate the relationship between feeding and our life with God.

To learn more about the responsibility involved in eating and sharing with others.

1. Starting out: what have we got?

Preparation

You will need paper, pens, flip chart or board and a calendar.

If your place of worship has a social or events committee or group, invite someone from that group to your session to contribute to the discussion

- Ask the group to think about what kinds of social events take place in your community which involve food? These events can also include non-church events. Make a list of such events against a calendar.

  Ask the group

  ○ How many people outside the church are involved in such occasions?

  ○ What would it take to offer more hospitality to more sections of the community?

  ○ In what ways can a connection be made between sharing food and God's love for people?

  Make a plan with your group to add at least *one* more social event to the life of your church or fellowship.

2. Going deeper: exploring flavours

Preparation

Ask people to bring in a selection of foods or drinks with different tastes. For example, ask for a selection of different teas or coffees, wines, sweets, biscuits, fruits or spicy foods. You can just have a range of Pot Noodle if you like!

- Invite group members to try a little of each and to write down the different flavours in order of preference.

- Invite group members to share their preferences and to explore why some people prefer one kind of flavour to another. Ask the group to think further about whether your place of worship has a 'flavour' (eg denomination, style of worship, church tradition).

  🍀 **What could be done to accommodate people who don't like the 'taste' of church?**

- You could also have a blindfold tasting of the various foods and invite the group to consider:
  - How easy are different foods to identify by taste? Do any particular foods stand out?
  - What do you think is the distinctive taste (or 'salt 'or 'leaven') of Christian faith in your own community?

3. Entering the world of the hungry
Preparation

Tell the group beforehand that you are organising a fast day. If you don't already hold family fast days in your church or fellowship you should give guidance on what to do and invite people to go without food as appropriate to their age and health. This might mean going without food completely, or reducing to one meal, eating smaller meals, or ask people to give up tea, coffee or other favourite drink for that day.

- Organise a fast day for the group. Ask people to come to the session feeling hungry

  Place some food (eg a few pieces of fruit or pieces of cake etc) in the centre of the group and have it as a centrepiece throughout the discussion.

  In pairs, invite people to share their experiences of times when they have gone without food – perhaps in war time or before an operation.

  After this time of sharing ask people to stop and listen to their bodies. What does talking about food in the presence of food do to our physical bodies? Invite people to notice their hunger and how they feel.

  At the conclusion of this activity, throw the food away without allowing anyone to eat it. Invite the group to discuss how they feel about wasting the food.

- As a result of raising awareness through this exercise, you could ask the group to help organise further fast days for your church or fellowship in which the money saved from not eating for a day is donated to an aid agency of your choice.

4. Reaching out to others: providing refreshment
Preparation

In advance of the session give everyone in your group the task of making some snacks (cakes or biscuits, chapattis, pies, etc) and sharing it with someone they know, as a gift to a neighbour or a friend, or for people at work.

- Invite the group to discuss in pairs what it was like to make the food and what reactions they got from sharing it. Invite the whole group to discuss together how the activity made people feel?
- Ask the group to suggest locations, events and times when it would be possible to offer simple refreshments to people outside the church (eg visitors coming to your church, social events, school events etc).

Organise at least *one* further occasion when visitors or people you don't know, could be offered hospitality.

5. Celebrating being Church together: Feasting
Preparation

Organise a party, either in someone's home or by asking members of the group each to bring a contribution to a shared meal, or by organising a fish and chip supper, an Agape meal or some other celebration.

● This is intended to be a purely social and hospitable occasion. There is no outcome to this meal – just allow everyone to enjoy themselves.

● If you prefer, you could set the celebration within a worship context by organising the party to take place after a celebration of Holy Communion.

6. Praying together
Preparation

Decide what pilgrimage you would like to do and ask a couple of group members in advance to set up the refreshment, eg tea and cake or juice and crisps.

● Use the church pilgrimage at http://wordbytes.org/holyland/index. html or construct a short pilgrimage around your own church and surrounding area with short prayers to use at each stop. There is material to help you do this on our website. ⊕ Invite everyone to pause at the end of the pilgrimage and share in refreshment.

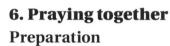

Journey Points for Imagination

Purpose of the journey

To learn about the power and possibility of imagination, wondering and dreaming;

To learn more about the imagination of others;

To encounter others creatively and to find ways to share faith.

1. Starting out: what have we got?
Preparation

You will need a number of everyday objects eg a bucket, a cheese grater, a mousetrap, a dog's lead, etc – about twice as many objects as there are people in the group. Try to include some objects relating to church life – a hymn book or a gift envelope.

The never-ending story

● With the group sitting in a circle, place the objects in the centre. Ask each person to choose an object and to spend five minutes thinking about it – what the object is, where it comes from, what might be done with it. Ask each person in turn to begin a story about his or her object. After about a minute, or sooner, if people begin to dry up, ask the next person to continue the story but to bring in their own object.

After everyone has told the story of their object, ask people how they felt about the exercise.

○ Were some objects easier to deal with imaginatively than others?

○ Did the group want to continue the story or to reach some sort of proper ending or conclusion?

○ Was the exercise fun or hard work?

2. Going deeper: The game of the gift
Preparation
You will need an 'unpleasant' object such as a bloody knife/axe from a joke shop or other toy store. Make sure the object looks as if it has been involved in violence. You can also do this game with a 'magic' ring.

● Seat members of the group in a circle. Indicate at the beginning that there are no right or wrong answers in playing the game. The rules of the game are that each person in turn must hold the object. Beginning with the first person, each person offers the knife as a 'gift' to the next person. No one may refuse the gift but must treat the object as a gift from a friend, thank their friend for the gift and say what they might do with it before passing it on. This can also be done by miming or role play.

Without attributing the comments to individuals, make a list of what people said they would do with the knife (wash it, get rid of it, give it to police etc).

Check to see if anyone during the game spoke about using the knife in a violent way. If not, why did people want to avoid the violence of the knife?

● Another version of this interesting game is to use a 'magic' ring. Play the game as in the knife example, but invite people to say what they would do with a magic ring.

Make a list of what people suggested would be uses for a magic ring. Were all the suggested uses 'good' uses? Would anybody be tempted to use the ring for personal gain, but said the 'right' thing anyway?

🗩 Invite the group to discuss whether handling these objects and talking about them was uncomfortable and if so why?

3. Entering the world of fading memory
Preparation
You will need information for a memory task, and if you wish collect pictures of film stars and/or pop singers for a visual display. If you do the second activity you will need to use a pub quiz book or download a suitable quiz or mixture of quizzes from the internet. Try to use a wide range of categories.

● Divide the group into pairs and give everyone a memory task. The task could be to write down all the verses of a long hymn, or to recall

the plot of a well known film including the names of all the actors and the names of the characters they played. Alternatively, display pictures of film stars or pop singers past and present and ask people in pairs to identify them *and* name what films they starred in or the names of their hit singles.

> 🗨 **Ask people to review their results. What did people do with any gaps, leave them blank? Guess? Make something up?**

● Get the group to do a pub quiz together by organising teams which are as mixed as possible in age range. Or you can organise a team game of *Trivial Pursuit* or *Who Wants to be a Millionaire*? There is an interactive pub quiz about Jesus on the rejesus website www.rejesus. co.uk.

> 🗨 **Ask group members to reflect on the questions they didn't know the answers to or couldn't quite remember. How did the team co-operate to find the answers?**

> 🗨 **Ask the group to discuss what they would feel like if they did not know any of the answers or remember any the details.**

4. Reaching out to others: other people's stories
Preparation

Collect a set of magazine/newspaper photographs of unknown people (eg advertisement models) or ask the group members to bring in a selection of photographs which include a number of people in the background. A holiday video will do as well.

● Invite group members to concentrate on one person in the background and imagine what they are doing there. Build up an imaginary profile of the person:

○ What is the person called?

○ Who are they with?

○ Why are they there?

○ What are they doing?

○ How are they feeling?

○ What is their life like?

○ What dreams do they have?

○ Where might they be a year's time?

The purpose of this process is to explore what it takes to turn strangers into friends and to examine the empathic process. Ask the group members to remember this exercise when they next make friends with a stranger or newcomer.

5. Celebrating being Church together
Preparation

This section contains larger and more extensive activities using imagination resources. You can choose a single book or a film or a bible study for the exploration of imagination in this journey, but these activities can also be extended beyond the group and are supported by materials on the website.🌐

Start a film club

Choose a suitable film or TV episode and allow enough time for people to watch and enjoy it together. Encourage people to discuss the themes, issues and ideas of the film afterwards. Draw out any themes and issues which are important to Christians.

Form a Reading Group

Choose a suitable book and give people at least a week to read the book. (In a regular reading group, you might want to meet at monthly or quarterly intervals). Encourage people to discuss the themes, issues and ideas of the book afterwards. Draw out any themes and issues which are important to Christians.

Imagining through Bible Study

The basis of the *Godly Play* experience is 'I wonder....' Choose a well known bible story and read through it in the group. Ask the group then to imagine the *back story* to what happens in the chosen story, where had the people just come from when they appear in the story, who had they talked to earlier in the day, what things had happened on the way to the story and what happens to them afterwards. This can be done as role play if you prefer.

Invite the group to consider how an invitation to wonder and dream can make bible study more creative and interesting.

6. Praying together: making a labyrinth
Preparation

Using pieces of paper or card as stepping stones, construct a simple labyrinth in the form of a spiral, ending at a central point marked by a chair. While people are walking the labyrinth, it can help to dim the lights and have some quiet music playing in the background. If you do this exercise with care, the labyrinth might be reusable, repeatable or could be scaled up as a resource for your whole congregation.

Ask the group to agree some simple images representing matters for prayer relevant to your particular church. Get members of the group to draw the images on to the stones.

Make some time for the group to walk the spiral one by one, praying through the issues marked by the images on the stones. Invite people to pause for about half a minute at the chair before leaving the labyrinth.

More about us

The Mission Theological Advisory Group

Dr Anne Richards is National Adviser: mission theology, alternative spiritualities and new religious movements in the Mission and Public Affairs Division of the Archbishops' Council of the Church of England. She has been secretary of MTAG since 1992, overseeing other MTAG publications such as *The Search for Faith and the Witness of the Church, Presence and Prophecy* and *Transparencies*.

Dr Nicholas Adams is Lecturer in Systematic Theology and Theological Ethics, New College, Edinburgh University. He is interested in German philosophy's influence on theology (esp. Kant, Jacobi, Hamann, Fichte, Hegel, Schelling, Schleiermacher), Frankfurt School Critical Theory, Non-Global Christian Ethics and theological reflections on music. His latest book is on Jurgen Habermas and theology.

The Rt Revd Dr David Atkinson became Suffragan Bishop of Thetford in the Anglican Diocese of Norwich in 2001. He taught chemistry and religious studies before training for ordination. He has written a number of books including *Counselling in Context* (with Francis Bridger), *Jesus, Lamb of God; God So Loved the World (towards a missionary theology)* and *Pastoral Ethics*.

Mr Simon Barrow is Co-Director of the Christian think-tank Ekklesia, and works as a freelance writer and consultant on religion and public life. He was formerly Commission Secretary for the Churches' Commission on Mission at Churches Together in Britain and Ireland.

Mr Andrew Brookes is a Roman Catholic based in Wantage, Oxfordshire, and has been engaged, in a variety of roles, in the fields of mission and ecumenism in, and sometimes beyond, the UK. He is the author of *The Alpha Phenomenon*.

Rt Revd Dr Brian Castle is suffragan bishop of Tonbridge in the Anglican diocese of Rochester. He has worked in Lesotho, South Africa, and Zambia as well as at the World Council of Churches and Cuddesdon theological college. He is also the Archbishop's adviser on alternative spiritualities and new religious movements. He has a particular interest in hymns and music. He is the author of *Unofficial God?*

Revd Professor John Drane is the author of such works as *The McDonaldization of the Church, What is the New Age Still Saying to the Church?* and *Biblical Faith and Cultural Change*. He is also an adjunct professor of theology at Fuller Seminary. His research interests are particularly focused on contemporary spirituality in popular culture and its implications for the church's mission and worship.

The Revd Canon Dr Graham Kings is Vicar of St Mary's Islington, a Vice-President of the Church Mission Society, a member of the Liturgical Commission and the theological secretary of Fulcrum. Previously he was the founding Director of the Henry Martyn Centre for the study of mission and world Christianity in the Cambridge Theological Federation and affiliated lecturer in the Faculty of Divinity, University of Cambridge and Vice-Principal of St Andrew's Theological College, Kabare, Kenya.

The Revd Canon Joanna Penberthy is a parish priest responsible for a number of village churches in the St David's diocese of the Church in Wales. She has served on the Council for Mission and Ministry for the Church in Wales and is Warden for Readers. She has been involved in a number of the Churches' Commission on Mission's projects and interests.

Revd Dr Israel Selvanayagam is a minister of the Church of South India. After many years teaching religions, mission and inter faith dialogue at Tamil Nadu Theological Seminar, Madurai, he was appointed World Church Tutor at Wesley College, Bristol and then at Queen's College, Birmingham. He was Principal of The United College of the Ascension.

Revd Dr David Spriggs is the Bible Society's Head of Church and Mission Group. His role involves engaging churches on national and local levels with the opportunities which Bible Society's campaigning initiatives provide. He is also involved in many national groups, which are concerned with helping churches become more missional. David is an ordained Baptist minister and has served in three full-time pastorates, the last in the City Centre Church in Coventry.

Revd Dr Andrew Wood is Chair of the Southampton District of the Methodist Church. He was also the Convenor of Interface – a Methodist group which explores the relationship between faith & contemporary culture.

Canon Janice Price heads up the Global Mission Network (formerly Churches' Commission on Mission) of Churches Together in Britain and Ireland. She has also been National Mission and Evangelism Adviser for the Church of England and Director of Development for the Anglican Diocese of Worcester. She is the author of *Telling Your Faith Story*.

Journey's Endnotes

Preface notes

1 This was a voluntary question and answered by 92% of people. See National Statistics online at www.statistics.gov.uk.
2 See, for example, statistics provided by the Church of England at www.cofe. anglican.org/info/statistics.
3 For example, David Hay and Kate Hunt, *The Spirituality of People who don't go to Church*, University of Nottingham 2000 available at www.ctbi.org.uk.
4 Sermon at Church Army Admitting Service 8th July 2004.

Introduction notes

1 For a book taking us on a journey through such wonders, see Michael Mayne, *This Sunrise of Wonder, A quest for God in art and nature*, Fount 1995. Also see Esther de Waal, *Lost in Wonder: Rediscovering the Spiritual Art of Attentiveness*, Canterbury Press 2003.
2 So *Godly Play*, by Jerome Berryman, for example, sets out a worship experience for children which specifically invites wonder, exploration and dreaming within the unfolding of sacrament. See Jerome Berryman, *Godly Play, an imaginative approach to religious edu*cation, Augsburg Fortress (paperback edition) 1995.
3 This story is told in 'The Case of the Colour-Blind Painter' in *An Anthropologist on Mars*, Picador 1995. Sacks is very interested in colour-blindness and has published another book entitled *The Island of the Colour-blind*, Picador 1996.
4 Brian Keenan, *An Evil Cradling*, Vintage edition 1993, pp. 68–9.
5 Julian of Norwich, *Revelations of Divine Love*, chapter 5.
6 Nick Spencer, *Beyond Belief? Barriers and Bridges to Faith Today*, LICC 2004.
7 St Irenaeus, *Against Heresies* 4.20.7.

Journey into Seeing notes

1 See *The Ancestor's Tale, Pilgrimage to the Dawn of Life*, Weidenfeld and Nicholson, 2004, p 128 and the whole section on colour vision, pp. 125–130.
2 David Jones, 'A, a, a, Domine Deus', from *The Sleeping Lord and other Fragments*, Faber and Faber 1974, p. 9.
3 You can see more of these at http://www.at-bristol.org.uk/Optical/default.htm.
4 *In the Beginning There Was Darkness: A Blind Person's Conversations with the Bible* SCM 2001. See also John Hull's *On Sight and Insight: A Journey into the World of Blindness*, Oneworld 1997, reprinted 2001.
5 http://www.fortunecity.com/emachines/e11/86/blind.html.
6 See http://www.users.totalise.co.uk/~tmd/color.htm.
7 http://www.sarahsarchangels.com/archangels/info.html.
8 LICC 2004, p. 22.
9 www.vanishingtattoo.com/tattoo/celeb-beckham.htm.
10 For example, see Richard Taylor's *How to Read a Church: A Guide to Images, Symbols and Meanings in Churches and Cathedrals*, Rider, 2003
11 See James Joyce, *Ulysses*, Penguin edition, 1969, p. 82.
12 *Ponder these Things, praying with icons of the Virgin Mary*, SCM, Canterbury Press, 2000, and *The Dwelling of the Light, praying with icons of Christ*, SCM Canterbury Press, 2004.
13 See http://www.wibsite.com/goodfriday/locations/cookham2004/2.htm for one such project.
14 Based on the Spiritual Exercises of St Ignatius of Loyola.

Journey into Hearing notes

1 David Hay and Kate Hunt, *The Spirituality of People who don't go to Church, University of Nottingham*, 2000, p. 39.
2 *Word in Action*, Summer 2004, p. 9.
3 David Hay and Kate Hunt, *Understanding the Spirituality of people who don't go to church*, University of Nottingham 2000, p. 13.
4 In 'Four Quartets', *Complete Poems and Plays of T S Eli*ot, Faber and Faber 1969, p. 192.
5 From a keynote speech given at a seminar for teachers of 'Special Education Needs' students. See http://www.evelyn.co.uk/disabled.htm
6 http://www.zak.co.il/deaf-info/index-abbrev.html under 'deaf art'.
7 From Dominican Life Today USA, the online news magazine of the Dominicans (Order of Preachers). Visit them at www.domlife.org.
8 *P!nk, God is a DJ*, BMG (single) 2004.
9 See http://www.delirious.co.uk.

10 *A House Divided*, interview at http://www.christianitytoday.com/music/interviews/2004/grits-0704.html
11 Robin A Leaver, *Music as Preaching: Bach, Passions and Music in Worship*, Latimer Studies 13, Oxford 1982, p. 31.
12 So 'Reel Christmas' was a success in Manchester along with its associated campaign 'Sing for the lad'.
13 From *Mean Time*, Anvil Press Poetry, 1993, p. 52.

Journey into Smell notes

1 Oliver Sacks, 'The Dog Beneath the Skin' in *The Man who Mistook his Wife for a Hat*, Picador edition 1986, p 150.
2 Aldous Huxley, *Eyeless in Gaza*, Penguin edition 1955, p. 50.
3 Factsheet from Fleur Aromatherapy http://www.fleur.co.uk/ess_oils_what.html?
4 Aldous Huxley, *Eyeless in Gaza*, Penguin edition 1955, p. 33.
5 Aldous Huxley, *Eyeless in Gaza*, Penguin edition 1955, p. 17.
6 Reported in *Metro*, 20 September 2004, p. 3.
7 Aldous Huxley, *Eyeless in Gaza*, Penguin edition 1955, p. 26.
8 Aldous Huxley, *Eyeless in Gaza*, Penguin edition 1955, p. 114.

Journey into Touching notes

1 See Colin Buchanan's Grove booklet, *The Kiss of Peace*, 1982
2 Mark Haddon, *The Curious Incident of the Dog in the Night-Time*, Jonathan Cape 2003, pp. 8–9.
3 *The Curious Incident of the Dog in the Night-Time*, p. 21.
4 In the story 'An Anthropologist on Mars' in the book of the same name, Picador 1995, pp. 233–82.
5 http://www.anglicancommunion.org/acns/articles/39/00/acns3912.cfm
6 From http://www.metta.org.uk/therap/indian_head_massage.htm.

Journey into Tasting notes

1 'The Bitter Herb' is a tale of Rebbe Nachman of Breslov. See for instance, www.breslov.org/stories.
2 Jenny Spouge, 'God of Rice and Chapatti' in *Harvest for the World*, compiled by Geoffrey Duncan for Christian Aid and CAFOD, Canterbury Press, 2nd edition 2004, p. 234.
3 William L Wallace, 'Behind and Within' in *Harvest for the World*, compiled by Geoffrey Duncan for Christian Aid and CAFOD, Canterbury Press, 2004 edition, p. 224.
4 John Diamond, *C*, Vermilion 1998, p. 157.
5 John Diamond, *C*, Vermilion 1998, pp. 201–2.
6 Redmond O'Hanlon, *In Trouble Again: A Journey Between the Orinoco and the Amazon*, Penguin, 1988, p. 176.
7 Redmond O'Hanlon, *In Trouble Again*, 1988, p. 230.
8 Marina O'Loughlin, restaurant review, *Metro* newspaper 3 March 2004, p. 21.
9 Delia Smith, *Delia's How to Cook, Book Two*, BBC Worldwide Limited, London 1999, p. 13.
10 Spurlock has some interesting comments at http://www.iofilm.co.uk/feats/interviews/s/morgan_spurlock_super_size_me.php
11 Jean-Paul Sartre, *Nausea*, Penguin edition 1965, p. 162.
12 David Ford, *The Shape of Living*, Fount (HarperCollins) 1997, pp. 168–9.

Journey into Imagination notes

1 David Hay and Kate Hunt, *Understanding the Spirituality of People who don't go to Church*, University of Nottingham 2000, p 21.
2 David Jones, *The Sleeping Lord and other fragments*, Faber 1974, p86.
3 For example, see Peter Millar, former warden of the Iona community, *Our Hearts Still Sing*, Wild Goose Publishing, 2004.
4 A helpful book is *Changing Minds, our lives and mental illness*, Gaskell Publications 2002, edited by Rosalind Ramsay, Anne Page, Tricia Goodman and Deborah Hart.
5 Erin's story at http://www.dbsalliance.org/Stories/Erin.html.
6 Office of National Statistics at http://www.statistics.gov.uk.
7 Go via http://www.shipoffools.com/church/ to see what happened to this experiment.
8 There are also online versions of the prayer journey. For example, http://www.yfc.co.uk/labyrinth/online.html.

Acknowledgements

The group is grateful to David McLeod of Makar Publishing Production for the design and layout of this book. Thanks also to Caroline Pratt for helping us with the permissions. Thanks also go to Revd Canon Bob Fyffe, General Secretary of CTBI for supporting this project.

Text Credits

The group is grateful to the following for permission to quote from published work:

Extracts from: *An Evil Cradling* by Brian Keenan, published by Hutchinson. Reprinted by permission of The Random house Group Ltd;

C: because cowards get cancer too by John Diamond, published by Vermilion. Reprinted by permission of the Random House Group Ltd.

The Curious Incident of the Dog in the Night-Time by Mark Haddon, published by Jonathan Cape. Reprinted by permission of The Random House Group.

The Archbishop of Canterbury's Christmas Message 2004 by kind permission of Lambeth Palace and the ACNS.

Blackwell Publishers for permission to quote from *The Spiritual Revolution* by Paul Heelas and Linda Woodhead.

Professor Richard Dawkins for permission to quote from *The Ancestor's Tale*.

The Dominicans (Order of Preachers)for permission to quote from their online news magazine Dominican Life Today USA at www.domlife.org.

'Prayer' is taken from *Mean Time* by Carol Ann Duffy published by Anvil Press Poetry in 1993.

Faber and Faber for permission to quote from David Jones, *The Sleeping Lord and other fragments*.

Faber and Faber for permission to quote from T S Eliot, *Collected Poems*.

Robin Leaver and Latimer House, for permission to quote *from Music as Preaching, Bach, Passions and Music in Worship*.

Pan Macmillan for permission to quote from *The Man who Mistook his Wife for a Hat* by Oliver Sacks.

Margaret Millard and Fleur Aromatherapy Limited for permission to quote from their website.

Mark Craig and www.metta.org.uk for permission to reproduce material on Indian Head Massage.

Penguin Books for permission to quote from Redmond O'Hanlon's *In Trouble Again*.

Penguin Books for permission to quote from Jean-Paul Sartre's *Nausea*.

Nick Spencer and the London Institute of Contemporary Spirituality for permission to quote from *Beyond Belief*.

'God of Rice and Chapatti' © Jenny Spouge from *Harvest for the World* compiled by Geoffrey Duncan and published by the Canterbury Press.

'Behind and Within' copyright W. L. Wallace from *Harvest for the World* compiled by Geoffrey Duncan and published by the Canterbury Press.

Emma Kay for permission to reproduce *Receiving Grace*, and also by kind permission of the owners Professor Tak and Mrs Andree Lee.

Silvia Dimitrova and the Revd Canon Dr Graham Kings for permission to reproduce Silvia's *Rabbouni* and Graham's poem of the same name.

Miriam Kings for permission to reproduce her 'Christ of Clothes'.

List of works cited

Ian M Banks, *Look to Windward*, Orbit, 2000.

Jerome Berryman, *Godly Play, an imaginative approach to religious edu*cation, Augsburg Fortress (paperback edition) 1995.

Dan Brown, *The Da Vinci Code*, Doubleday, 2003.

Walter Brueggemann, *Prophetic Imagination*, Fortress Press 1978.

Colin Buchanan *The Kiss of Peace*, Grove booklet 1982.

CMS, *The Christ we Share*, pack available from the Church Mission Society.

Richard Dawkins, *The Ancestor's Tale, Pilgrimage to the Dawn of Life*, Weidenfeld and Nicholson, 2004.

Esther de Waal, *Lost in Wonder: Rediscovering the Spiritual Art of Attentiveness*, Canterbury Press 2003.

John Diamond, *C*, Vermilion 1998.

Carol Ann Duffy *Mean Time*, Anvil Press Poetry 1993.

Geoffrey Duncan (ed) *Harvest for the World*, compiled for Christian Aid and CAFOD, Canterbury Press, 2nd edition 2004.

T S Eliot, *Complete Poems and Plays of T S El*iot, Faber and Faber 1969.

David Ford, *The Shape of Living*, Fount (HarperCollins) 1997.

Mark Haddon, *The Curious Incident of the Dog in the Night-Time*, Jonathan Cape 2003.

Paul Heelas, Linda Woodhead etc *The Spiritual Revolution, why religion is giving way to spirituality*, Blackwell, 2004.

Walter Hilton, *The Ladder of Perfection*, Kessinger Publishing 2004.

David Hay and Kate Hunt, *The Spirituality of People who don't go to Church*, University of Nottingham 2000.

John Hull, *In the Beginning There Was Darkness: A Blind Person's Conversations with the Bible* SCM 2001.

John Hull *On Sight and Insight: A Journey into the World of Blindness*, Oneworld 1997, reprinted 2001.

John Hull book *Touching the Rock*, Vintage, reprint edition 1992.

Aldous Huxley, *Eyeless in Gaza*, Penguin edition 1955.

David Jones, *The Sleeping Lord and other Fragments*, Faber and Faber 1974.

James Joyce, *Ulysses*, Penguin edition 1969.

Julian of Norwich, *Revelations of Divine Love*, Penguin Classics, New Ed edition 1999.

Carl Gustav Jung, *The Meaning of Psychology for Modern Man*, 1934.

Patrick Kavanagh, *Collected Poems*, Penguin Classics 2005.

Brian Keenan, *An Evil Cradling*, Vintage edition 1993.

C S Lewis *Narnia* series.

Ignatius Loyola, *The Spiritual Exercises*, Paulist Press 1991.

Michael Mayne, *This Sunrise of Wonder, A quest for God in art and nature*, Fount 1995.

Peter Millar, *Our Hearts Still Sing*, Wild Goose Publishing, 2004.

Redmond O'Hanlon, *In Trouble Again, a journey between the Orinoco and the Amazon*, Penguin, 1988.

Philip Pullman, *His Dark Materials*, Trilogy edition, Scholastic Press 2001.

Rosalind Ramsay, Anne Page, Tricia Goodman and Deborah Hart. (eds) *Changing Minds, our lives and mental illness*, Gaskell Publications 2002.

Alain Robbe-Grillet, *La Jalousie*, Methuen Educational 1969.

Russ Parker, *Healing Dreams* Triangle 1993.

Russ Parker, *Dream Stories*, BRF 2002.

Oliver Sacks, *The Man who Mistook his Wife for a Hat*, Picador edition 1986.

Oliver Sacks, *An Anthropologist on Mars*, Picador 1995.

Oliver Sacks *The Island of the Colour-blind*, Picador 1996.

Jean Paul Satre, *Nausea*, Penguin edition 1965.

Shakespeare, *Othello*.

Christopher Smart, *Selected Poems*, Penguin Classics 1990.

Delia Smith, *Delia's How to cook*, book two, BBC Worldwide Limited, London 1999.

Nick Spencer, *Beyond Belief? Barriers and Bridges to Faith Today*, LICC, 2004.

David Spriggs, *Feasting on God's Word*, Bible Reading Fellowship, 2003.

St Irenaeus, *Against Heresies* , Kessinger Publishing 2004.

Patrick Süskind *Perfume*, Penguin edition 1987.

Richard Taylor *How to Read a Church: A Guide to Images, Symbols and Meanings in Churches and Cathedrals*, Rider, 2003.

JRR Tolkien *The Silmarillion* Del Ray, reissue 1995.

Rowan Williams, *Ponder these Things, praying with icons of the Virgin Mary*, SCM, Canterbury Press 2000.

Rowan Williams, *Silence and Honey Cakes*, Lion Publishing 2003.

Rowan Williams, *The Dwelling of the Light, praying with icons of Christ*, SCM Canterbury Press 2004.

Image credits

All reasonable efforts have been made to obtain permission to reproduce material from sources. In the event of a query, please contact the publisher.

Cover, shutterstock_3226703 double spiral fractal ©Bobbie Sandlin.

p.i shutterstock 2506182 nautilus outer shell ©Dee Golden.

p.iv shutterstock 2681931 glass globe ©David H. Seymour.

p.v shutterstock 1651350 Union Jack ©John Rawsterne; shutterstock 101843 English flag ©Dimitrios Kaisaris; shutterstock 3534655 Scottish Flag ©Steven Kratochwill; shutterstock 1842852 Welsh flag ©Carsten Reisinger; shutterstock 101811 Irish Flag ©Dimitrios Kaisaris; shutterstock 4044499 abstract cross ©Daniela Illing.

p.vi shutterstock 1777663 dna model ©Sebastian Kaulitzki; shutterstock 2762089 toy windmill ©Carlos Caetano; shutterstock 2100477 boy and telescope ©Nick Stubbs; shutterstock 2134557 microscope ©Jakub Semeniuk; shutterstock 1645215 snail ©Grzegorz Slemp.

p.vii shutterstock 2148065 dna model ©Shebanov Alexandr; shutterstock 1194673 virus ©sgame; shutterstock 2966229 red blood cells ©James Steidl.

p.viii, xi abstract earth *anon*.

p. ix, nut and bolt morguefile; shutterstock 1413475 paper clips ©sgame.

p. x, shutterstock 2227996 web internet icon ©aranzazu cueva santa nacher mulet *ff*; *The Creation of the World*, closed doors of the triptych *The Garden of Earthly Delight*, c.1500 by Hieronymous Bosch, Museodel Prado, Madrid.

p.xii-1, Whirlpool galaxy, January 2005. NASA, ESA, S. Beckwith (STSel), and the Hubble Heritage Team (STScl/AURA).

p.1, *La Creazione del Mondo*, by Giusto de'Menabuoi, c.1350. Baptistry of Padua Cathedral, northern Italy.

p.2, shutterstock 1710391 sun vector ©Rzymu; Colossus of Rhodes, wood engraving reconstruction by Sidney Barclay c.1875 supplied by Historical Pictures Service in Chicago in Encyclopedia Britannica Concise; shutterstock 1162749 stained glass light ©Sue; Shutterstock 86842 Stonehenge ©Alex Melnick.

p.3, shutterstock 110467 pottery ©Hashim Pudiyapura.

p.4, shutterstock 2440054 dna doublehelix ©Yakobchuk Vasyl; orange and lime morguefile; Mother Julian of Norwich *anon*; shutterstock 2435299 hazelnuts ©Jovan Nikolic.

p.5, Equilibrium ©Mirimax/Dimension Films.

p.6, shutterstock 2851053 abstract eye ©Dusan Jankovic; shutterstock 2896442 whisper vignette ©Melanie DeFazio; shutterstock 2059466 beggar ©Arman Zhenikeyev.

p.7, shutterstock 1804697 communion ©James Steidl; shutterstock 1320480 fuzzy eye chart ©Tomasz Trojanowski.

p.8, Mary anointing feet of Jesus free Christian web clipart.

p.9, shutterstock 1659893 worship concert ©Donald Linscott.

p.10, shutterstock 4535545 3D-DNA ©Sai Yeung Chan; shutterstock 2671920 Eiffel Tower ©Mike Liu.

p.11, eye morguefile *anon*.

p.12, shutterstock 2321029 coloured pencils ©Rafa Irusta;

shutterstock 754219 lamp and bible ©Radim Strojek.

p.13, shutterstock King of Kings 1655338 ©Lisa Howard; shutterstock 2795414 binoculars ©Maciej Oleksy.

p.14, Fraser and other spirals after Nicholas Wade, *The Art and Science of Visual Illusions*, Rourledge & Kegan Paul, 1982.

p.15, shutterstock 1891099 Bible braile ©Karin Lau; shutterstock 865034 blind man walking ©PhotoCreate.

p.16, shutterstock 2091152 storm clouds and cross ©Bruce Rolff; shutterstock 2798924 cloud light after storm ©ANP; shutterstock 2949648 multimedia icons ©Alexander Lukin.

p.17, shutterstock 2130396 Mandelbrot fractal ©Douglas Greenwald; shutterstock 3430152 double rainbow ©Dusan Po.

p.18, shutterstock 2921482 palette of lipstick ©Andrey Chmelyov; shutterstock 1597349 yoga pose ©Alfred Wekelo; shutterstock 2402944 anorexic image ©Linda Bucklin; shutterstock 2850676 keyhole eye ©Dusan Zidar.

p.19, shutterstock 1667801 don't look ©Mark E. Stout; shutterstock 1036046 webcam ©André Klaassen; shutterstock 779264 cctv camera ©Hugo Maes

p.20, shutterstock 3062590 rosary ©Michal Rozanski; shutterstock 1175777 fisheye broadway church ©emin kuliyev.

p.21, shutterstock 1135139 abbey light ©sean Elliott; Emma Kay – *Receiving Grace*.

p.22, icon of the Trinity painted around 1410 by Andrei Rublev.

p.23, shutterstock 1697078 rooftop crosses ©David Mcke; shutterstock 1668444 shopping centre ©Ewa Walicka.

p.24, shutterstock 3627932 magnifying glass ©Joel Calheiro; shutterstock 1307243 x-ray ©kuehdi; shutterstock 1986080 remote control ©Vinicius Tupinamba; shutterstock 435560-1 looking eyes ©Hisom Silviu.

p.25, shutterstock 2764858 flute and clarinet ©Robynrg.

p.26, shutterstock 2678003 soundwave ©Sebastian Kaulitzki; shutterstock 2133356 cartoon music score ©Gabor Palkovics; shutterstock 2093345 violin ©Lebedinski Vladislav Evgenievitch; shutterstock 300318 old time radio ©J. Helgason.

p.27, morguefile 154685 church bells ©xander; morguefile clock 132522 ©ladyheart; shutterstock 2289141 listen up ©Andres Rodriguez.

p.28, shutterstock 1018711 angel choir ©Mary Terriberry; shutterstock 2676929 Gospel of St John ©Milos Luzanin.

p.29, shutterstock 2164521 young preacher ©Dennis Owusu-Ansah; shutterstock 3053970 I can't hear you ©Mikael Damkier; shutterstock 1956045 talk gently ©Artsem Martysiuk.

p.30, shutterstock 773669 bible in candleight ©Lincoln Rogers; shutterstock 2818697 fishers of men stained glass window ©V. J. Matthew.

p.31, shutterstock 2988614 woman praying ©Alexander Motrenko; shutterstock 2218534 young girl praying ©Dennis Owusu-Ansah.

p.32, shutterstock 1855240 hearing aid ©Oktay Ortakcioglu; shutterstock 2679895 sign language ©Robert Adrian Hillman; shutterstock 32397 0K sign ©Dan Thomas Brostrom.

p.33, shutterstock 1830823 mp3 player ©Elena Aliaga; shutterstock 147300 buddhist meditation hand ©Radu Razvan.

p.34, shutterstock 2965029 dj ©James Thew; shutterstock 2631082 christian dancer ©Kiselev Andrey Valerevich.

p.35, shutterstock 2427082 rock star scream ©Darko Novakovic; shutterstock 220299 church organ ©Steffen Foerster Photography.

p.36, shutterstock 1447933 girl chilling ©Daniel Sroga; noisy girl *anon*.

p.37, guitar morguefile anon; shutterstock 2634035 female choir singer ©Ken Hurst; Russian church choir morguefile *anon*.

p.38, shutterstock 1315216 praying man ©Christa DeRidder; shutterstock 1774883 violin and score ©paolo jacopo medda; shutterstock 2603526 cupid with trumpet ©Orrza; shutterstock 718652 angel decoration with harp ©Villedieu Christophe; shutterstock 320271 angel ornament with harp

©Carolina K. Smith.

p.39, shutterstock 2991130 global music ©Norebbo; shutterstock 2990760 Beverly Knight ©Jason Bennee; shutterstock 630219 Elton John and gospel singers ©Massimiliano Lamagna.

p.40, shutterstock 1761569 dove ©Brian Erickson; shutterstock 752604 hymn board ©SueC; morgufile ref 66348 choirbook © anita patterson.

p.41, shutterstock 3233169 exhuberant youth ©Andresr; shutterstock 1551964 choir singer ©Ken Hurst.

p.43, shutterstock 2957597 young girl with flower ©maribell.

p.44, shutterstock 2987248 blue fragrance stream ©cloki.

p.45, shutterstock 2028970 baby bathing ©Tjerrie Smit; shutterstock 2817226 smelly ©matka Wariatka.

p.46, shutterstock 3042355 perfume bottle ©Pierre Yu; shutterstock 2913982 lotion and flowers ©lukacs racz; shutterstock 2917683 dead foliage ©Sebastian Knight; shutterstock 2866625 smoke © Ivan Tsvetkov Petrov; shutterstock 3013052 decaying leaf ©iconex.

p.47, shutterstock 2894778 ivy ©Kateryna Potrokhova; shutterstock 597154 ©Alexander; shutterstock grapes 2103312 ©Michal Kolosowski; shutterstock 2950205 shoes ©Ersler Dmitry.

p.48, shutterstock 2959245 candle and cross ©Oleinik Dmitri.

p.49, shutterstock 2497466 incense ©Norman Chan.

p.50, shutterstock 764549 stuffy nose ©Jamie Wilson.

p.51, shutterstock 3030779 aromatherapy ©Michelle Marsan.

p.52, shutterstock 673997 dirty ashtrtay ©Michele Perbellini; shutterstock 2828729 disinfectant ©Elena Schweitze; shutterstock 2874392 spa arrangement ©MaxFX.

p.53, shutterstock 2456801 doorway to dreams ©Niserin; shutterstock 2154020 cigarette smoke ©Wallenrock.

p.54, shutterstock 2847035 skeleton ©Vova Pomortzeff.

p.55, shutterstock 1379372 ironing ©Dóri O'Connell; shutterstock 2954862 sunflower ©Constant; shutterstock 2525022 popcorn ©OlgaLis.

p.56, shutterstock 1520636 © Black Ink Designers, Corp.; shutterstock 2898348 roast dinner ©Joe Gough; shutterstock 2071680 grass ©Fribus Ekaterina.

p.57, shutterstock 1897667 lavendar ©Cre8tive Images.

p.58, shutterstock 2762209 bread ©Thomas M Perkins; shutterstock 3025404 green wisps of smoke ©Anyka.

p.59, shutterstock 2594515 tulip ©cloki.

p.61, shutterstock 2308386 touch ©Killroy Productions.

p.62, shutterstock 2580888 palm through tissue paper to yelogreen ©Quayside; shutterstock 987117 snake and apple ©Alex James Bramwell; shutterstock 1922526 garden spider ©Susan McKenzie; shutterstock 1104273 fingers ©Filipe Raimundo.

p.63, shutterstock 2131694 braille ©prism 68; shutterstock 1003601 baptism ©vadim kozlovsky; shutterstock 402962 hands in dirt ©Varina and Jay Patel;

p.64, shutterstock 235202 pebbles ©Marcus Tuerner; shutterstock 1150531 celtic stone cross ©Alfio Ferlito; shutterstock 1861618 touch trumpet ©Scott Rothstein; shutterstock 504008 kid in kitchen ©Suzanne Tucker.

p.65, sistine chapel hands *anon*.

p.66, shutterstock 751178 crucifixion ©George Bailey; shutterstock 474943 floating hand ©Chris Harvey; shutterstock 1064585 taking communion ©Suzanne Tucker.

p.67, shutterstock 2818947 hands gripped©Peter Baxter; shutterstock 2126777 thumbprint ©Ismael Montero Verdu; shutterstock 822156 cancer patient and her husband sharing a tender moment of affection ©Lisa F. Young.

p.68, shutterstock 2268191 syringe and blood ©Gnuskin Petr; shutterstock 1786919/2281299 roaches ©Robert Adrian Hillman ©Marcus M. Jones; shutterstock 2427951 head massage ©Yanik Chauvin.

p.69, shutterstock 2245680 back off ©Robert Adrian Hillman; Shutterstock 2584751 abused woman ©Stephanie Swartz; shutterstock 1898400 fists ©Artsem Martysiuk; shutterstock 2386789 reach out ©Artsem martysiuk.

p.70, doctor *anon*; shutterstock 3033162 hairdresser and client ©Marin; shutterstock 3035915 doctor and girl ©Steve Cole; shutterstock 3049849 dentist vignette©Nemanja Glumac.

p.71, shutterstock 2689969 head massage ©Alfred Wekelo.

p.72, shutterstock 1527200 pedicure ©Dewayne Flowers; shutterstock 1096953 botox injection ©Leah-Anne Thompson; shutterstock 1801145 high heels ©Ternovoy Dmitry.

p.73, shutterstock 897862 tattoo ©Ryan Klos; touching Jesus – The Incredulity of St Thomas *c.*1620 by Bernardo Strozzi (Compton Verney House Trust [Peter Mores Foundation]).

p.74, shutterstock 2640369 bridal gown ©Gordana Sermek; shutterstock 868876 old black boots ©Liette Parent; shutterstock 2922611 father–child hands touching ©Radkevich Siarhei.

p.75, shutterstock 2177331 air kiss ©Dan Thomas Brostrom; Miriam King installation; Morguefile f145370 clergy ©darnok; shutterstock 1984455 Dahlai Lama ©Vova Pomortzeff; shutterstock 811136 trendy minister ©Timothy Large.

p.76, shutterstock 2888179 red silk ©emily2k; shutterstock 2020221 Gethsemane reconstruction ©Glenda M. Powers.

p.77, shutterstock 2456284 sewing kit ©Goran Kuzmanovski; shutterstock 1451076 paint streaks ©Henning Janos; shutterstock 2097032 fuschia scarf ©Joellen L Armstrong.

p.78, shutterstock 2384408 hands through tissue ©Franziska Richter.

p.79, shutterstock 1294927 tasty ice lolly cropped ©Anette Linnea Rasmussen.

p.80, shutterstock 2762080 red wine pouring into glass ©Tischenko Irina; shutterstock 822833 salt shaker ©Hatem Eldoronki; shutterstock 1095145 brown sugar in spoon ©Ewa Brozek; shutterstock 2745462 lemons ©Szymon Apanowicz; shutterstock 2589667 instant coffee ©Marek Szumlas;

p.81, shutterstock 1794420 liquids in glasses ©Konstantin Andryukhin; shutterstock 2515309 baby sucking thumb ©Melanie DeFazio; shutterstock 3067433 honeycomb ©Christina Tisi-Kramer.

p.82, shutterstock 1940681 eat words ©Gina Goforth; shutterstock 1855081 bitter medicine ©Studio Araminta; shutterstock 1122504 broken bread ©jeff gynane; shutterstock 280519 salt spoon ©tadija; shutterstock 3019599 microscopic salt granules ©Constantine Vishnevsk.

p.83, shutterstock 3083098 grapes ©Maksim Shmeljov; shutterstock 2243122 sour lime ©Kirk Peart Professional Imaging; shutterstock 695149 horseradish ©Milos Luzanin.

p.84, shutterstock 2840740 radish ©Jovan Nikolic; shutterstock 2480343 food at last supper ©Justin Kirk Thornton; shutterstock 2029440 slab of beef ©Leonid Nishko.

p.85, shutterstock 2841545 fire ©David Lee; shutterstock 2970786 lamb ©Eric Isselée; shutterstock 846216 impoverished African children ©Geir Olav Lyngfjell.

p.86, shutterstock 2545824 rice bowl ©Doreen Salcher; shutterstock 2701056 wheat in hand ©Zaichenko Olga; shutterstock 470076 saying grace ©Lisa F. Young.

p.87, shutterstock 2082974 communion ©Magdalena Kucova; Morguefile 159461 rice paddy ©chilombiano; shutterstock 3052532 atom ©Michael Osterrieder; shutterstock 1873985 recycle world ©Jerome Scholler.

p.88, shutterstock 3117747 half pear ©Alex Star.

p.89, shutterstock 2318992 feet ©Mudassar Ahmed Dar; shutterstock 3117254 can of worms ©Ed Endicott–Wysiwyg Foto LLC; shutterstock 2680314 roast potatoe ©Andy Butler.

p.90, shutterstock 3018516 champagne pop ©Nikola Bilic; shutterstock 2685536 kidney ©David Romero Corra; shutterstock 2629527 bowl of soup ©Timothy Geiss; shutterstock 2892862 food alpha ©Olga Lyubkina.

p.91, shutterstock 2719738 knife and fork ©bluestocking; shutterstock 2650018 sushi ©mashe; shutterstock 549892 chef at work ©Tonis Valing; Maldon sea salt chez McLeod ©Makar.

p.92, shutterstock 953207 salt label ©Robert Pernell; shutterstock 2668620 water wave ©Adam Borkowski; shutterstock 3080092 bottled water poured ©Ljupco

Smokovski; shutterstock 2540038 fat man ©David Gaylor.

p.93, shutterstock 1013247 food pryamid ©Olga Lyubkina; shutterstock 442134 healthy senior ©Graca Victoria.

p.94, shutterstock 109547 bad apple ©Scott Rothstein; shutterstock 2518561 dollar coffee ©Steve Smith; FAIRTRADE registered logo.

p.95, shutterstock 2604734 grub ©Thomas M Perkins; shutterstock 2791251 burger ©Thomas M Perkins; Mr Creosote from *The Meaning of Life*, ©1983 Universal City Studios; shutterstock 3049163 cone ©Robyn Mackenzie; shutterstock 2502022 chocolate bar ©Rafa Irusta.

p.96, shutterstock 1915292 Qu'ran fast ©Paul Cowan; shutterstock 1963335 turkish delight ©Paul Cowan.

p.97, shutterstock 1596730 chef ©Antonis Papatoniou; shutterstock 1843144 pasta shells ©Lein de León Yong.

p.98, shutterstock 2623450 rosemary ©sierpniowka; shutterstock 1799300 hot chilli peppers ©Peter Doomen; shutterstock 1927531 watermelon ©Pichugin Dmitry; shutterstock 154975 noodles ©Johanna Goodyear.

p.99, shutterstock 498997 radial labyrinth ©Bruce Rolff.

p.100, shutterstock 3258751 vapordream ©Tomas Smolek; shutterstock 2234308 compact disc ©Carlos E. Santa Maria; shutterstock 3081764 notepad and pencil ©Tatiana Popova; shutterstock 2606028 bible ©Lukasz Kwapien; shutterstock 2920161 ace cards ©Kasia; shutterstock 3236473 chessboard ©Vorobyev Denis; shutterstock 2335069-1 saxaphone ©Izaokas Sapiro.

p.101, shutterstock 2666977 rose tinted glasses ©David H.Seymour; shutterstock 3104873 thoughtful girl ©Denis Pogostin; shutterstock 3049278 sailboat sunset ©Eric Gevaert; shutterstock 2457067 depressed man ©Kevin Carden; shutterstock 1289052 golden egg ©sgame.

p.102, shutterstock 3126904 floating doorway ©appler; shutterstock 3130116 pyramid ©Kulish Viktoriia.

p.103, shutterstock 2698684 ghosts ©Dejan Lazarevic; shutterstock 1321306 father and son ©Suzanne Tucke.

p.104, shutterstock 2619772-1 pilgrims ©Jozef Sedmak; shutterstock 2635939 child's hands praying ©Thomas M Perkins.

P.105, shutterstock 2295127 pregnant ©Christophe Testi; shutterstock 2442481 sea shell ©kristian; shutterstock 3248020 orchid ©Brian Chase.

P.106, shutterstock 2867344 dna man ©Gudron; shutterstock 2406163 woman praying ©Laurin Rinde; shutterstock 2440871 pills ©Agb.

p.107, shutterstock 934910 crying woman ©Andrija Kova; shutterstock 1316769 depressed man ©Olga Lyubkina.

p.108, shutterstock 834198 family reading Bible together ©Jaimie Duplass; shutterstock 2311470 chocolates ©Thomas M Perkins; shutterstock 1224139 cryptex ©Amy Walters; shutterstock 1211525 open book ©Neven Mendrila.

p.109, shutterstock 1986184 fractal nebula ©anajka; shutterstock 834687 braincell and fetal man ©Scott Maxwell.

p.110, shutterstock 1931276 world in digital hand ©Antonis Papantoniou; shutterstock 2701711 intense female stare ©Victoria Alexandrova.

p.111, shutterstock 1515102 admit one ©George Pappas; shutterstock 2883920 movie screen montage ©Christos Georghiou/Makar; Donnie Darko ©Newmarket Films/Flower Films.

p.112, shutterstock 3189012 open door ©Tyler Boyes.

p.113 Rabbouni ©Silvia Dimitrova.

p.114, details from Rabbouni ©Silvia Dimitrova; shutterstock 2052307 labyrinth vector ©NP.

p.115, shutterstock 838876 handpuppet ©Laura Neal.

p.116, shutterstock 1777675 dna spiral ©Sebastian Kaulitzki.

p.117, shutterstock 183762 footprints ©Elena Ray;

p.118, shutterstock 1957511 christian music concert ©Mike Flippo.

p.119, shutterstock 2401515 dove ©Christopher Ewing.

p.120, shutterstock 916157 dna concept background ©Nicemonkey.